AF413145

THE LATE WAR

Between the United States and Great Britain

Rogershaven Facsimile Edition

Originally Published in
New York, 1819
by Daniel D. Smith

Published By
ROGERSHAVEN BOOKS

The Late War
Rogershaven Facsimile Edition

Inquiries should be addressed to
Inquiries@RogershavenBooks.com

ISBN: 979-8-8692-4427-7

STEPHEN DECATUR ESQR.E

of the United States Navy.

Engraved for Hunts History of the War

THE
LATE WAR,

BETWEEN THE

UNITED STATES AND GREAT BRITAIN,

From June, 1812, to February, 1815.

WRITTEN IN THE ANCIENT HISTORICAL STYLE.

BY GILBERT J. HUNT.

" The good of his country was the pride of his heart."
.Decatur's victory.

CONTAINING, ALSO, A SKETCH OF THE LATE

ALGERINE WAR;

And the Treaty concluded with the Dey of Algiers
Commercial Treaty with Great Britain,
and the Treaty concluded with the
Creek Nation of Indians.

THIRD EDITION.

With improvements by the author.

New-York:

PUBLISHED BY DANIEL D. SMITH,
No. 190, Greenwich-Street.

1819.

PREFACE.

THE advantages which the introduction of this work into our seminaries of education would be likely to produce are many and obvious:

1. The author having adopted for the model of his style the phraseology of the best of books, remarkable for its simplicity and strength, the young pupil will acquire, with the knowledge of reading, a love for the manner in which the great truths of Divine Revelation are conveyed to his understanding, and this will be an inducement to him to study the Holy Scriptures.

2 All the circumstances related in this work are true; they are recent, being within the recollection of the present generation; they form a very important part in the history of our country, and will be read with pride and pleasure by every one of our young men in whose bosom may glow the sentiments of patriotism and piety.

3. The most prominent virtues of the heroes who produced the events here treated of, are held up in such a manner as to inspire in the youthful mind a love for the country they defended, and a spirit of honorable emulation, which may be highly advantageous to that country whenever it shall be necessary to call it into exercise.

4. Although a vein of morality runs through the work, the sentiments have not the smallest bearing on the particular tenets of any religious sect, but are calculated to be read by all persons, of whatever denomination, who love virtue, valor, and freedom.

5. The facts described are related in so clear and concise a way as without much effort on the part of the pupil, will easily fasten themselves on his memory.

These are some amongst other reasons which have induced the author to recommend his little work to

teachers of youth throughout the United States, as
well as fathers of families, and he does it in the confi-
dent hope, that it will prove useful in accelerating the
progress of knowledge, and in awakening and cherish-
ing in the minds of his young countrymen those prin-
ciples of virtue with which he has been careful that it
should be interwoven.

Having received the universal approbation of men
of judgment, he only thinks it necessary to give the
following letters from Dr. S. L. Mitchill, and Mr.
Picket.

G. J. HUNT.

New-York, June 13, 1817.

Sir,

I had noticed your work on the late war long
before I had the pleasure of your acquaintance. It
seems to be a plain and popular mode of exhibiting the
transactions of which it treats.

One of the defects in the literature of our country
is that of good historians. That class of our citizens
which is called to act, shows unparalleled atchievement
and enterprize. The other sections, to whom is allot-
ted the business of narrating and recording events, are
not so far advanced, the reason is evident; there must
be deeds to describe and perpetuate, before there can be
historians. In process of time, writers duly qualified,
will make their appearance.

Your Chronicle of events deserves to be mentioned
in the list of useful publications. It will answer as a
document of constant and ready reference. The reception of it into schools, will render familiar to children the chief actions in the contest, and teach them, at
the same time, to respect their country and its institu-
tions.

It seems to me one of the best attempts to imitate
the biblical style; and if the perusal of it can induce
young persons to relish and love the sacred books

whose language you have imitated, it will be the strongest of all recommendations.

Your's respectfully.
SAMUEL L. MITCHILL.

Mr. G. J. Hunt.

Academy, New-York, July 8, 1817.

Sir,

I have examined the copy, and concur in the
recommendation of the publication of your " Historical Reader, with the alterations and improvements, for
the Use of Schools. I sincerely hope that your exertions
may be crowned with success.

Your's respectfully,

Mr. G. J. Hunt.
J. W. PICKET.

TABLE OF CONTENTS.

TABLE OF CONTENTS. vii

THE HISTORY

OF THE

LATE WAR

BETWEEN THE

U. STATES AND G. BRITAIN,

CHAP. I.

President's Message—Causes of the War—Energetic Measures proposed.

Now it came to pass, in the one thousand eight hundred and twelfth year of the christian era, and in the thirty and sixth year after the people of the provinces of Columbia had declared themselves a free and independent nation;

2 That in the sixth month of the same year, on the first day of the month, the chief Governor, whom the people had chosen to rule over the land of Columbia;

3 Even JAMES, whose sir-name was MADISON, delivered a written paper to the GREAT SANHEDRIM of the people, who were assembled together.

4 And the name of the city where the people were gathered together was called after the name of the chief captain of the land of Columbia, whose fame extendeth to the uttermost parts of the earth; albeit, he had slept with his fathers.

B

5 Nevertheless, the people loved him, forasmuch as he wrought their deliverance from the yoke of tyranny in times past; so they called the city WASH-INGTON.

6 Now, when the written paper was received, the doors of the chambers of the Great Sanhedrim were closed, and a seal was put upon every man's mouth.

7 And the counsellors of the nation, and the wise men thereof, ordered the written paper which James had delivered unto them to be read aloud; and the interpretation thereof was in this wise:

8 Lo! the lords and the princes of the kingdom of Britain, in the fulness of their pride and power, have trampled upon the altar of Liberty, and violated the sanctuary thereof:

9 Inasmuch as they hearkened not unto the voice of moderation, when the cry of the people of Columbia was, Peace! peace!

10 Inasmuch as they permitted not the tall ships of Columbia to sail in peace on the waters of the mighty deep; saying in their hearts, Of these will we make spoil, and they shall be given unto the king.

11 Inasmuch as they robbed the ships of Columbia of the strong men that wrought therein, and took them for their own use, even as a man taketh his ox or his ass.

12 Inasmuch as they kept the men stolen from the ships of Columbia in bondage many years, and caused them to fight the battles of the king, even against their own brethren! neither gave they unto them silver or gold, but many stripes.

13 Now the men of Columbia were not like unto

the men of Britain; for their backs were not harden-
ed unto the whip, as were the servants of the king;
therefore they murmured, and their murmurings have
been heard.

14 Moreover, the Council of Britain sent forth a Decree to all the nations of the earth, sealed with the signet
of the Prince Regent, who governed the nation in the
name of the king his father; for lo! the king was pos-
sessed of an evil spirit, and his son reigned in his stead.

15 Now this Decree of the Council of Britain was
a grievous thing, inasmuch as it permitted not those who
dealt in merchandize to go whithersoever they chose, and
to trade freely with all parts of the earth.

16 And it fell hard upon the people of Columbia;
for the king said unto them, Ye shall come with your
vessels unto me and pay tribute, then may ye depart to
another country.

17 Now these things pleased the pirates and the
cruisers of Britain mightily, because it permitted them to
rob the commerce of Columbia with impunity.

18 Furthermore, have not the servants of the king
leagued with the savages of the wilderness, and given
unto them silver and gold, and placed the destroying engines in their hands?

19 Thereby stirring up the spirit of Satan within
them, that they might spill the blood of the people of
Columbia; even the blood of our old men, our wives,
and our little ones!

20 Thus, had Britain, in her heart, commenced War
against the people of Columbia, whilst they cried aloud
for peace: and when she smote them on the one cheek
they turned unto her the other also.

21 Now, therefore, shall we, the independent people of Columbia, sit down silently, as slaves, and bow the neck to Britain?

22 Or, shall we, like our forefathers, nobly assert our rights, and defend that LIBERTY and INDEPENDENCE which the Lord hath given unto us?

CHAP. II.

Report of the Committee—Declaration of War.

Now, when there was an end made of reading the paper which James had written, the Sanhedrim communed one with another touching the matter :

2 And they chose certain wise men from among them to deliberate thereon.

3 And they commanded them to go forth from their presence, for that purpose, and return again on the third day of the same month.

4 Now, when the third day arrived, at the eleventh hour of the day, they came forth and presented themselves before the Great Sanhedrim of the people.

5 And the chief of the wise men, whom they had chosen, opened his mouth and spake unto them after this manner :

6 Behold ! day and night have we meditated upon the words which James hath delivered, and we are weary withal, for in our hearts we desired peace.

7 But the wickedness of the kingdom of Great-Britain, and the cruelty of the princes thereof, towards the peaceable inhabitants of the land of Columbia, may be likened unto the fierce lion, when he putteth his paw upon the innocent lamb to devour him.

8 Nevertheless, the lamb shall not be slain; for the Lord shall be his deliverer.

9 And if, peradventure, the people of Columbia go

not out to battle against the king, then will the manifold wrongs committed against them be increased tenfold, and they shall be as a mock and a bye-word among all nations.

10 Moreover, the righteousness of your cause shall lead you to glory, and the pillars of your liberty shall not be shaken.

11 Therefore, say we unto you, Gird on your swords and go forth to battle against the king; even against the strong powers of Britain; and the Lord God of Hosts be with you.

12 Now when the great Sanhedrim of the people heard those things which the wise men had uttered, they pondered them in their minds many days, and weighed them well;

13 Even until the seventeenth day of the month pondered they in secret concerning the matter.

14 And it was so, that on the next day they sent forth a DECREE, making WAR upon the kingdom of Great Britain, and upon the servants, and upon the slaves thereof.

15 And the Decree was signed with the hand writing of JAMES, the chief Governor of the land of Columbia.

16 After these things, the doors of the chambers of the Sanhedrim were opened.

CHAP. III.

Reception of the Declaration of War in Great Britain —her friends in America—Caleb Strong—Hartford Convention.

———

AND it came to pass, that when the princes and the lords and the counsellors of Britain saw the Decree, their wrath was kindled, and their hearts were ready to burst with indignation.

2 For, verily, said they, this insult hath overflowed the cup of our patience; and now will we chastise the impudence of these Yankees, and the people of Columbia shall bow before the king.

3 Then will we rule them with a rod of iron; and they shall be, unto us, hewers of wood and drawers of water.

4 For, verily, shall we suffer these cunning Yankees to beard the mighty lion, with half a dozen fir-built frigates, the men whereof are but mercenary cowards— " bastards and outlaws ?"

5 Neither durst they array themselves in battle against the men of Britain. No ! we will sweep them from the face of the waters, and their name shall be heard no more among nations.

6 Shall the proud conquerors of Europe not laugh to scorn the feeble efforts of a few unorganized soldiers, undisciplined, and fresh from the plough, the hoe, and the mattock ?

7 Yea, they shall surely fall; for they were not bred to fighting as were the servants of the king.

8 Their large cities, their towns, and their villages will we burn with consuming fire.

9 Their oil, and their wheat, and their rye, and their corn, and their barley, and their rice, and their buckwheat, and their oats, and their flax, and all the products of their country will we destroy, and scatter the remnants thereof to the four winds of heaven.

10 All these things, and more, will we do unto this froward people.

11 Neither shall there be found safety for age or sex from the destroying swords of the soldiers of the king ;

12 Save in those provinces and towns where dwell the friends of the king , for, lo ! said they, the king's friends are many.

13 These will we spare; neither will we hurt a hair of their heads : nor shall the savages of the wilderness stain the scalping-knife or the tomahawk with the blood of the king's friends.

14 Now it happened, about this time, that there were numbers of the inhabitants of the country of Columbia whose hearts yearned after the king of Britain.

15 And with their false flattering words they led astray some of the friends of COLUMBIAN LIBERTY; for their tongues were smoother than oil.

16 Evil machinations entered into their hearts, and the poison of their breath might be likened unto the deadly Bohon Upas, which rears its lofty branches in the barren valley of Java.*

---

* *Of the existence of this wonderful tree there have been doubts : but the reader is referred to the relation of P. N. Foerch, who has given a satisfactory account of it, from his own travels in its neighbourhood.*

17 And they strove to dishearten the true friends of the great Sanhedrim; but they prevailed not.

18 Moreover, Satan entered into the heart of one of the governors of the east, and he was led astray by the wickedness thereof, even *Caleb the Strong*.

19 Now Caleb, which in the Cherokee tongue, signifieth an ass, liked not the decree of the great Sanhedrim, inasmuch as he favored the king of Britain;

20 And, though willing to become a beast of burden, yet would he not move on account of his very great stupidity.

21 And he said unto the captains of the hosts of the state over which he presided, Lo! it seemeth not meet unto me that ye go forth to battle against the king.

22 For, Lo! are not the fighting men of Britain, in multitude, as the sand on the sea shore? and shall we prevail against them?

23 Are not the mighty ships of the king spread over the whole face of the waters? Is not Britain the " bulwark of our religion?"

24 Therefore, I command that ye go not out to battle, but every man remain in his own house.

25 And all the governors of the east listened unto the voice of Caleb.

26 Moreover, the angel of the Lord whispered into the ear of Caleb, and spake unto him, saying,

27 If, peradventure, thou dost refuse to obey the laws of the land, the thing will not be pleasant in the sight of the Lord;

28 Inasmuch as it may cause the people to rise up one against another, and spill the blood of their own children;

29 And the time of warfare will be lengthened out, and the blood of thousands will be upon thine head.

30 And Satan spake, and said unto Caleb, Fear not ; for if thou wilt forsake thy country, and throw off the paltry subterfuge of COLUMBIAN LIBERTY, and defy the councils of the great Sanhedrim,

31 Then shall thy name be proclaimed with the sound of the trumpet throughout all the earth ; and thou shalt be a prince and a ruler over this people.

32 Now the smooth words of Satan tickled Caleb mightily, and he hearkened unto the counsel of the wicked one :

33 For the good counsel given unto him was as water thrown upon a rock.

34 But when the chief governor and the great Sanhedrim of the people saw the wickedness of Caleb, their hearts were moved with pity towards him and his followers : yea, even those who had made a convention at the little town of Hartford.

35 Neither doth the scribe desire to dwell upon the wickedness which came into the village of Hartford, the signification of the name whereof, in the vernacular tongue, appeareth not.

36 For the meddling therewith is as the green pool of unclean waters, when a man casteth a stone therein.

CHAP. IV.

John Henry—Elijah Parish.

LET the children of Columbia beware of false prophets which come in sheep's clothing; for it is written,
Ye shall know them by their fruits.

2 Now it came to pass, that a certain man, whose sir-
name was Henry, came before James, the chief governor, and opened his mouth, and spake unto him, saying,

3 Lo! If thou wilt give unto me two score and ten
thousand pieces of silver, then will I unfold unto thee the
witchcraft of Britain, that thereby thy nation may not be
caught in her snares.

4 And James said unto him, Verily, for the good of
my country I will do this thing.

5 And immediately the man Henry opened his mouth,
a second time, and said,

6 Lo! the lords and counsellors of Britain have
made a covenant with me, and have promised me many
pieces of gold if I would make a league with the provinces of the east that they might favour the king; and
long and faithfully have I laboured in their cause.

7 But they deceived me, even as they would de-
ceive the people of Columbia; for their promises are
as the idle wind that passeth by, which no man re-
gardeth.

8 And, when he had gotten the silver into his own

hands he departed to the land of the Gauls, where he re-maineth even until this day.

9 Nevertheless, the people profitted much thereby; inasmuch as it put them upon the watch, and they guarded themselves against the evil accordingly.

10 He that longeth after the interpretation of the deeds of Henry, let him make inquiry of those who acted with him—the ministers of the Hartford Convention.

11 Now, there was a certain hypocrite, whose name was Elijah, and he was a false prophet in the east, and he led astray those of little understanding; moreover, he was an hireling, and preached for the sake of filthy lucre.

12 And he rose up and called himself a preacher of the gospel, and his words were smooth, and the people marvelled at him;

13 But he profaned the temple of the Lord, and he strove to lead his disciples into the wrong way.

14 And many wise men turned their backs against him; nevertheless, he repented not of his sins unto this day.

15 Neither did the people, as Darius the Mede did unto the prophet Daniel, cast him into the den of lions, that they might see whether the royal beast would disdain to devour him.

16 But they were rejoiced that power was not given unto him to command fire to come down from heaven to consume the friends of the great Sanhedrim.

CHAP. V.

American Army—Militia—Navy—British Navy—Rodgers' first Cruise—Capture of the U. S. brig Nautilus—removal of aliens beyond tide-water.

———◆———

THE whole host of the people of Columbia, who had been trained to war, being numbered, was about seven thousand fighting men.*

2 Neither were they assembled together; but they were extended from the north to the south, about three thousand miles.†

3 But the husbandmen, who lived under their own fig-trees, and lifted the arm in defence of their own homes, were more than seven hundred thousand, all mighty men of valor.

4 Now the armies of the king of Britain, are they not numbered and written in the book of Hume, the scribe? is not their name a terror to all nations?

5 Moreover, the number of the strong ships of the peaceable inhabitants of Columbia, that moved on the waters of the deep, carrying therein the destroying engines, which vomited their thunders, was about one score; besides a handful of " cock-boats;" with " a bit of striped bunting at their mast-head."

6 But the number of the fighting vessels of Britain was about one thousand one score and one, which bore the royal cross.

---

* *Standing army.*

† *From District of Maine to Mobile Bay and New-Orleans.*

7 And the men of war of Britain were arrayed in their might against the people of the land of Columbia.

8 Nevertheless, it came to pass, that about this time a strong ship of the United States, called the President, commanded by a skilful man whose name was Rodgers,

9 Sailed towards the island of Britain, and went nigh unto it, and captured numbers of the vessels of the people of Britain, in their own waters; after which she returned in safety to the land of Columbia.

10 And the people gave much praise to Rodgers, for it was a cunning thing; inasmuch as he saved many ships that were richly laden, so that they fell not into the hands of the people of Britain.

11 Moreover, it happened about the fifteenth day of the seventh month, in the same year in which the decree of the great Sanhedrim was issued, that a certain vessel of the states of Columbia was environed round about by a multitude of the ships of the king;

12 And the captain thereof was straitened, and he looked around him and strove to escape:

13 But he was entrapped and fell a prey to the vessels of the king; howbeit, the captain, whose name was Crane, tarnished not his honor thereby.

14 And the name of the vessel of the United States was called Nautilus.

15 Now, about this time, there was a law sent forth from the great Sanhedrim, commanding all servants and subjects of the king of Britain forthwith to depart beyond the swellings of the waters of the great deep; even two score miles.

16 And they did so; and their friends from whom they were compelled to flee, mourned for them many days.

CHAP. VI.

Hull's expedition—he enters Canada, and encamps at Sandwich—issues his Proclamation—retreats to Detroit.

———

NOW it was known throughout the land of Columbia that war was declared against the kingdom of Britain.

2 And to a certain chief captain called William, whose sir-name was Hull, was given in trust a band of more than two thousand chosen men, to go forth to battle in the north.

3 Now Hull was a man well stricken in years, and he had been a captain in the host of Columbia, in the days that tried men's souls; even in the days of WASHINGTON.

4 Therefore, when he appeared in the presence of the great Sanhedrim, they were pleased with his countenance, and put much faith in him.*

5 Moreover, he was a governor in the north,† and a man of great wealth.

6 And when he arrived with his army hard by the Miami of the Lakes, he gat him a vessel and placed therein those things which were appertaining unto the preservation of the lives of the sick and the maimed.

7 But, in an evil hour, the vessel was ensnared, near unto a strong hold,‡ beside a river called in the language of the Gauls, Detroit.

———

* *Gen. Hull had been to Washington and obtained an appointment previous to the war.*
† *Michigan territory.*   ‡ *Malden.*

8 And the army of Columbia suffered much thereby.

9 Nevertheless, on the twelfth of the seventh month about the fourth watch of the night, William with his whole host crossed the river which is called Detroit.

10 And he encamped his men round about the town of Sandwich in the province of the king.

11 From this place, he sent forth a proclamation, which the great Sanhedrim had prepared for him ; and the wisdom thereof appeareth even unto this day.

12 But if a man's ass falleth into a ditch, shall the master suffer thereby ? if injury can be prevented, shall we not rather with our might endeavour to help him ?

13 Now in the proclamation which Hull published abroad, he invited the people of the province of Canada to join themselves to the host of Columbia, who were come to drive the servants of the king from their borders.

14 And it came to pass, that a great multitude flocked to the banners of the great Sanhedrim.

15 Nevertheless, they knew not that they were to be entrapt.

16 However, it was so, that William departed from the province of the king, and re-crossed the river.

17 And when the husbandmen of the province of Canada, who had joined the standard of Columbia, learned those things, they wept bitterly ; for they were left behind.

18 After this William secured himself in the strong nold of Detroit ; and the eyes of the men and the women of Columbia were fixed upon him.

19 And the expectation thereof may be likened unto a man who hath watered well his vineyard.

CHAP. VII.

Hull's expedition—surrender of his army and the whole Michigan Territory—his trial and pardon by the President—capture of Michilimackinack.

NOW the host of the king were few in numbers; nevertheless, they came in battle array against the strong hold of William.

2 And when he beheld them from afar, he was afraid; his knees smote one against another, and his heart sunk within him; for, lo! the savages of the wilderness appeared amongst them.

3 And there was a rumor went throughout the camp of Columbia, and it bore hard upon William.

4 Inasmuch as they said the wickedness of his heart was bent on giving up the strong hold to the servants of the king.

5 Howbeit he was not taxed with drinking of the strong waters of Jamaica; which, when they enter into the head of a man, destroy his reason and make him appear like unto one who hath lost his senses.

6 And when the charge against William was made known unto the soldiers of Columbia, they were grieved much, for they were brave men, and feared nought.

7 So the officers communed one with another touching the thing; but they wist not what to do.

8 And they fain would have done violence unto William, that they might have been enabled to pour forth their thunders against the approaching host of Britain; which he had forbidden to be done.

9 Moreover, the names of these valiant men, who were compelled to weep before the cowardice of William, are they not recorded in the bosom of every friend of Columbian liberty.*

10 And it was about the sixteenth of the eighth month when the servants of the king appeared before the strong hold of Detroit.

11 And the name of the chief captain of the province, of Canada, that came against the strong hold, was Brock, whose whole force was about seven hundred soldiers of the king, and as many savages.

12 Now when the soldiers of Canada were distant about a furlong, moving towards the strong hold; even when the destroying engines were ready to utter their thunders and smite them to the earth;

13 William, whose heart failed him, commanded the valiant men of Columbia to bow down before the servants of the king.

14 And he ordered them to yield up the destructive weapons which they held in their hands.

15 Neither could they appear in battle against the king again for many days.

16 Moreover, the cowardice of his heart caused him to make a league with the servants of the king, in the which he gave unto them the whole territory over which the people had entrusted him to preside; notwithstanding it appertained not unto him.

17 And the balls of solid iron, and the black dust, and the destroying engines became a prey unto the men of Britain.

18 Now there had followed after William a band of brave men from the west, and the name of their captain

---

* *Miller, Cass, M'Arthur, Brush, Findley, &c.*

was Brush; and he had in trust the bread and the wine which were to refresh the army of Columbia.

19 And, lest they should fall into the hands of the savages, a captain, whose name was Vanhorn, was ordered to go forth and meet him.

20 And the band that went forth, were entrapped at Brownstown, by the cunning savages, that laid wait for them; and the killed and the wounded of Columbia were about two score.

21 And again there were sent from the camp of William more than five hundred men to go to the aid of Brush.

22 And the name of the chief captain thereof, was Miller; and the captain whom he ordered to go before him was called Snelling.*

23 Now Snelling was a valiant man, and strove hard against the men of Britain, and the savages; even until Miller the chief captain arrived.

24 And the place which is called Maguago, lieth about an hundred furlongs from Detroit.

25 Now the battle waxed hot; and the host of Miller pressed hard upon the savages and upon the men of Britain.

26 Inasmuch as they were compelled to flee before the arms of Columbia: and Miller gat great honor thereby.

27 And there fell of the men of Britain that day an hundred two score and ten.

28 Nevertheless, in the league which William had made, he had included Miller, and all the brave captains and the men of war of Columbia that were nigh the place.

29 Now, therefore, whether it was cowardice out-

Col. Miller and Col. Snelling.

right, in William, or whether he became treacherous for filthy lucre's sake, appeareth not unto the scribe.*

30 But the effect thereof to the nation, was as a man having a millstone cast about his neck.

31 So William and his whole army fell into the hands of the servants of the king.

32 But, as it is written in the book of Solomon, There is a time for all things; so it came to pass, afterwards, that William was called to account for his evil deeds.

33 And he was examined before the lawful tribunal of his country; and they were all valiant warriors and chief captains in the land of Columbia.

34 Howbeit, when the council† had weighed well the matter, they declared him guilty of treason, and that he should suffer death.

35 Nevertheless, they recommended him to the mercy of James, the chief governor of the land of Columbia,

36 Saying, Lo! the wickedness of the man appeareth unto us as palpable as the noon day;

---

* *To palliate Hull's conduct, it has been urged that he surrendered his army to prevent the effusion of blood: but let us ask those charitable palliators what they would have said of Gen. Jackson, if, when a mighty and a blood-thirsty enemy appeared before his battlements, in quest of beauty and booty, he had given up N. Orleans and ceded the Louisiana territory to him? or of the gallant Croghan, when left to defend fort Stephenson with a handful of men and a single six pounder?—These palliators might even have wished that the heroes of Erie and Champlain had felt the same qualms of conscience:—but they ought to know that it was such noble deeds that stopt the "effusion of blood."*

† *Court-Martial.*

37 But the infirmities of his age have weakened his understanding; therefore let his grey hairs go down to the grave in silence.

38 And when James heard the words of the council, his heart melted as wax before the fire.

39 And he said, Lo! ye have done that which seemeth right unto me.

40 And although, as my soul hopeth for mercy, for this thing William shall not surely die; yet his name shall be blotted out from the list of the brave.

41 Notwithstanding this, William thanked him not, but added insult to cowardice.*

42 So William was ordered to depart to the land which lieth in the east,† where he remaineth unto this day: and his name shall be no more spoken of with reverence amongst men.

43 Moreover, there was another evil which fell upon the people of the United States, about the time the host of Columbia crossed the river Detroit.

44 For, lo! the strong hold of Michilimackinack, which lieth nigh unto the lakes of Michigan and Huron, fell an easy prey unto the men of Britain and their red brethren;

45 Whose numbers were more than four-fold greater than the men of Columbia, who knew not of the war.

46 Nevertheless, the people of the United States, even the great Sanhedrim, were not disheartened; neither were they afraid: for they had counted the cost, and were prepared to meet the evil.

---

* *Hull's address to the public.*   † *Massachusetts.*

CHAP. VIII.

*Capture of the British frigate Guerriere, by the United
State's frigate Constitution, captain Hull—capture
of the Alert sloop of war, by the Essex, captain
Porter.*

NOW it came to pass, on the nineteenth day of the
eighth month, that one of the tall ships of Columbia;
called the Constitution, commanded by Isaac, whose sir-
name was Hull,

2 Having spread her white wings on the bosom of the
mighty deep, beheld from afar one of the fighting ships
of Britain bearing the royal cross.

3 And the name of the ship was called, in the language of the French, Guerriere,* which signifieth a warrior, and Dacres was the captain thereof.

4 Now when Dacres beheld the ship of Columbia
his eyes sparkled with joy, for he had defied the vessels
of Columbia.

5 And he spake unto his officers and his men that
were under him, saying,

6 Let every man be at his post, and ere the glass hath
passed the third part of an hour the stripes of the Constitution shall cease to sweep the air of heaven,

7 And the yawning deep shall open its mouth to receive the enemies of the king.

---

* *The Guerriere was taken from the French by the
British.*

8 And the men of Dacres shouted aloud, and drank of the strong waters of Jamaica, which make men mad; moreover, they mixed the black dust therewith. —

9 Now when Isaac drew nigh unto the king's ship, the warriors of Columbia shouted.

10 And Isaac bore down upon the strong ship of the king.

11 About this time they put the lighted match to the black dust of the destroying engines, and it was like unto a clap of thunder.

12 Moreover, the fire and smoke issued out of the mouths of the engines in abundance, so as to darken the air, and they were overshadowed by the means thereof.

13 Now the black dust was not known among the ancients; even Solomon, in the plenitude of his wisdom, knew it not.

14 And the battle continued with tremendous roar for about the space of half an hour, when its noises ceased.

15 But when the clouds of smoke had passed away, behold! the mighty Guerriere lay a sinking wreck upon the face of the waters.

16 The shadow of hope passed over her as a dream; and most reluctantly was she compelled to strike the lion's red cross to the Eagle of Columbia:

17 Whilst the Constitution, like Shadrach in the fiery furnace, remaining unsinged, filled her white sails, and passed along as though nothing had happened unto her.

18 Now the slain and the maimed of the king that day were five score and five.

19 And the loss of the people of Columbia, was seven slain and seven wounded.

20 After this Isaac caused a burning coal to be placed in the Guerriere, that she might be consumed, and the flames thereof mounted towards the heavens.

21 And the great Sanhedrim honored Isaac with great honor, and the people were rejoiced in him, and they forgat, in the contemplation of his glory, the evils which had befallen them in the north.

22 But when the lords and counsellors of Britain heard those things, they believed them not; it was as the bitterness of gall to their souls: for the pride of Britain was fixed upon her navy; it was the apple of her eye.

23 Now, as one evil followeth after another to the sons of men, so it happened that, in the same month, a certain strong ship of the United States, even the Essex, the name of the captain whereof was Porter, sailed in search of the vessels of the king, on the waters of the ocean.

24 And in process of time, she fell upon one of the ships of Britain, called the Alert, and made spoil thereof to the people of Columbia.

CHAP. IX.

*Attack on Sacket's Harbour—affair of Ogdensburgh
—British drove from St. Regis, by the Troy militia
under major Young—the brigs Adams and Caledonia re-captured by capt. Elliot, near fort Erie.*

NOW the movements of the enemy were as the
motion of a whirlwind, which passeth from the north to
the south, and from the east to the west.

2 And they sought to encompass the whole land of
Columbia round about.

3 So it came to pass, that a number of the armed vessels of the king, that sailed on the great lake which is
called Ontario, moved towards Sacket's Harbour.

4 And they demanded certain vessels of the people
of the United States, which they had taken from the
king, to be given up unto them, saying,

5 Verily, if ye give them not up, then will we lay a
contribution upon you, and ye shall pay tribute.

6 But Bellinger, the chief captain of the Harbour,
refused.

7 And when the vessels of the king were hard by, a
certain captain, whose name was Woolsey, set one of the
engines to work.

8 And the vessels of the king also opened the mouths
of their engines, and shot into the camp of Columbia.

9 And the number of the husbandmen of the United

States that flocked to the defence of the Harbour was about three thousand.

10 And when the men of war of Britain saw that the people of Columbia were not afraid, and that they knew to use the destroying engines, they fled to their strong hold, in the province of the king, which is called Kingston.

11 Howbeit, some of their ships received much damage from the balls of heavy metal, that smote them from the strong hold.

12 Now as the malice of the nations increased one against another, so did the evils increase which surrounded them.

13 And it came to pass, on the fourth day of the tenth month, there came a thousand fighting men of Britain to lay waste the village of Ogdensburgh, which lieth hard by the river St. Lawrence.

14 Howbeit, the people of Columbia permitted them not to come unto the land ; but compelled them to depart in haste.

15 Nigh unto this place is a village which is called St. Regis, where the soldiers of Britain had come to fix a strong hold on the borders of Columbia.

16 But a brave captain, whose name was Young, with a band of men, called militia, went against them.

17 And he set the destroying engines to work, and the noise thereof sounded in their ears ; so they were discomfitted and fled in confusion.

18 And the number of the servants of the king, made captive that day, was two score men, with the instruments of destruction in their hands.

19 Moreover, one of the banners of the king, even

the red-cross standard of Britain, fell into the hands of Young.

20 On the eighth day of the same month, a captain of Columbia, whose name was Elliot, a cunning man, took a chosen band, who came from the sea-coast, and put them in boats.

21 And he departed with them from Niagara towards the strong hold of Erie, even in the dead of the night.

22 And he came unawares upon the two vessels which were covenanted to the king, with the army at Detroit.

23 And the names of the vessels were the Adams and the Caledonia, and Elliot captured them the same night.

24 However, the next day, as Elliot and his men were returning with their prizes, the men of Britain, who were upon the other shore, let the destroying engines loose upon them from their strong hold;

25 And a few of the people of Columbia were slain. It was here the valiant Cuyler* fell; a ball of heavy metal struck him as he was coming on a fleet horse towards the water's edge.

26 Now, Cuyler was a man well beloved; and the officers and men of Columbia grieved for him many days.

---

* *Major Cuyler of N. Jersey.*

CHAP. X.

Battle of Queenstown—the British General Brock killed.

AND it came to pass, on the morning of the thirteenth day of the tenth month,

2 That Stephen, a chief captain of Columbia, sirnamed Van Rensselaer, essayed to cross the river which is called Niagara, with his whole army.

3 Now the river lieth between the Lake Erie and the Lake Ontario.

4 And the noise of the waters of the river is louder than the roaring of the forest; yea, it is like unto the rushing of mighty armies to battle.

5 And the movement of the stupendous falls thereof bringeth the people from all parts of the earth to behold it.*

6 So Stephen gat his soldiers into the boats that were prepared for them, and they moved upon the rough waters of the river, towards the strong hold of Queenstown.

7 And when the men of Britain saw them approach, they opened the engines upon them, from Fort George, and round about.

8 Nevertheless, they persevered; although the strength of the waters, which were ungovernable, separated the army.

9 However, Solomon,† a captain and a kinsman of

----

* *Niagara Falls.*   † *Col. Solomon Van Rensselaer.*

Stephen, reached the shore with the men under his command, in all about two hundred.

10 And he put the army in battle array, in a valley, and moved up towards the strong hold; and Brock was the chief captain of the host of Britain.

11 And from their strong hold they shot, with their mischievous engines, balls of lead in abundance; and it was as a shower of hail upon the people of Columbia;

12 For there was no turning to the right hand nor to the left for safety.

13 And Solomon and his men fought hard; and they rushed into the hottest of the battle.

14 And a captain of the United States, whose name was Chrystie, followed close after them, with a chosen band of brave men.

15 So they pushed forward to the strong hold, and drove the men of Britain before them like sheep, and smote them hip and thigh with great slaughter; and Brock, their chief captain, was among the slain.

16 And Chrystie, and the valiant Wool, and Ogilvie, and the host of Columbia, got into the hold, and the army of the king fled: and Chrystie was wounded in the palm of his hand.

17 But Solomon was sorely wounded, so that his strength failed him, and he went not into the hold.

18 And that day there fell of the servants of the king many valiant men, even those who were called Invincibles, and had gained great honour in Egypt.

19 Nevertheless, the same day a mighty host of savages and soldiers of the king,* came forth again to battle,

---

* *Reinforcements from Fort George and Chippawa.*

and rushed upon the people of the United States, and
drove them from the strong hold of Queenstown.

20 For, lo! Stephen, the chief captain, could not prevail on the hosts of militia on the other side of the river
to cross over.

21 So the army of Columbia moved down towards
the river to cross over again, that they might escape.

22 But when they came down to the water side, lo!
they were deceived, for there was not a boat to convey
them to a place of safety; so they became captives to the
men of Britain.

23 Now the men of Britain treated the prisoners
kindly, and showed much tenderness towards them; for
which the people blessed them.

24 And the killed and wounded of the host of Columbia, were an hundred two score and ten.

25 And the prisoners that fell into the hands of the
king, were about seven hundred.

26 Nevertheless, in a letter which Stephen sent to
Henry,* the chief captain of the army of the north, he
gave great honor unto the captains who fought under
him that day.

27 And the names of the valiant men, who distinguished themselves in the battle, were Wadsworth, Van
Rensselaer, Scott, Chrystie, Fenwick, Fink, Gibson,
and many other brave men of war.

----

* *Major Gen. Dearborn.*

CHAP. XI.

Gen. Smyth succeeds Gen. Van Rensselaer—his attempt to cross the Niagara, and failure—causes.

AFTER these things, on the same day in which the letter was written, Stephen resigned the command of his army to a certain chief captain whose name was Alexander,*

2 Now Alexander was a man well skilled in the arts of warfare.

3 And he made a proclamation to the young men of the state of New York, wherein he invited them to go forth from their homes and join the host under him.

4 And the words thereof pleased the young men so that they went in numbers and joined Alexander, on the shores of the river which is called Niagara.

5 But here the hand of the scribe trembleth, his tongue faltereth, his heart sickeneth, and he would fain blot from his memory that which truth compels him to record ; for he is a living witness thereof.

6 Alas ! there was an evil spirit moving in secret and in bye-places throughout the land of Columbia.

7 And lo ! its viper-like insidiousness crept into the ears of the unwary husbandmen.

8 For the sect of the tories whispered unto them, saying, Lo! the laws of the land cannot compel you to step over the borders the United States.

---

* *Brig. Gen. Smyth.*

9 Moreover, said they, the fierceness of the savages is terrible as the wild tyger, and their numbers as the trees of the forest.

10 And the veteran soldiers of the king, who have been bred to war, are spread in multitudes over the province of Canada.

11 Therefore, if ye go over to fight against them, ye will be as sheep going to the slaughter; and ye shall never again return to the house of your fathers, for ye will be destroyed.

12 Even as the wickedness of the war, which the great Sanhedrim have made against the king cannot prosper, so shall ye fall a prey to the folly thereof.

13 And it came to pass when the husbandmen heard these smooth words, many of them were bewildered in their minds, and knew not what to do.

14 So when the young men, who had flocked to the banners of Alexander, came down to the waters edge, to go into the boats, they thought of the words which the enemies of Columbia had spoken unto them; and they refused to cross over:

15 Neither could the persuasions of the chief captain prevail on them all to go into the boats; and those whose hearts were willing were not enough.

16 So he was obliged to suffer them to return to their homes; for his expectations were blasted.

17 And the army of Columbia went into winter quarters; for the earth was covered with snow, and the waters of the great lakes, on the borders of which they had pitched their tents, were congealed.

CHAP. XII.

Capture of the British sloop of war Frolic, of 22 guns, by the United States' sloop of war Wasp, of 18 guns.

———

NOW the strong ships of war of the kingdom of Great Britain were spread over the whole face of the waters of the ocean.

2 But few, indeed, were the vessels of Columbia that were fighting ships, and carried the destroying engines.

3 Howsoever, early in the morning of the eighteenth day of the tenth month, about the sixth hour, being on the sabbath day,

4 One of the ships of Columbia, called the Wasp, the name of the captain whereof was Jones, a valiant man, discovered afar off one of the strong ships of the king.

5 Now the ship of Britain was mightier than the ship of Columbia; and she was called the Frolic, and the captain's name was Whinyeates.

6 And they began to utter their thunders about the eleventh hour of the day, and the noises continued for more than the space of half an hour;

7 When the Wasp, falling upon the Frolic, and getting entangled therewith, the men struggled together;

and the mariners of Columbia overpowered the mariners of Britain.

8 So it came to pass, that the Frolic became captive
to the ship of Columbia.

9 And the slain and the wounded of the king's ship
were about four score.

10 And the children of Columbia lost, in all, abou
half a score : howbeit, there was much damage done to
both vessels.

11 Nevertheless, about this time, a mighty ship o
Britain, called the Poictiers, came upon the vessels
which were in a defenceless situation, and took them
both, and commanded them to go to the island of the
king which is called Bermuda.

12 However, the people of Columbia were pleased
with the noble conduct of Jones, and for his valiant acts
they gave him a sword of curious workmanship.

13 Moreover, while he remained at Bermuda, the
inhabitants. the servants of the king, treated him kindly
and showed much respect for him and his officers the
were made captive.

CHAP. XIII.

Capture of the British frigate Macedonian, by Com. Decatur, in the frigate United States.—Brig Vixen captured by the British frigate Southampton.

NOW it happened on the twenty-fifth day of the tenth month, in the first year of the war; that a certain strong ship of Britain, that had prepared herself to fight a ship of Columbia, appeared upon the waters of the mighty deep.

2 And she was commanded by a valiant captain, whose name was Carden, and the name of the ship was the Macedonian.

3 And on the same day she met one of the strong ships of Columbia, the name of the captain whereof was Decatur, and the vessel was called tbe United States.

4 Now Decatur was a man who had never known fear; and the good of his country was the pride of his heart;

5 And when he came towards the vessel of the king, he used no entreaty with his men, for they all loved him, and the motion of his finger was as the word of his mouth.

6 So when the ships came nigh unto one another, their thunders were tremendous, and the smoke thereof was as a black cloud.

7 Neverthelcss, in the space of about ninety minutes,

the strong ship of Britain struck her red flag to the stripes of Columbia.

8 Now the Macedonian was a new ship and she gat much damage.

.9 But the United States, like the companions of Shadrach, moved unhurt upon the waters; nay, even her wings were not singed.

10 And the slain and the wounded, of the ship of the king, were five score and four.

11 And there fell of the people of Columbia five who were slain outright, and there were seven maimed.

12 Moreover the ship of Britain had seven of the stolen men of Columbia therein, who were compelled to fight against their brethren; and two of them were slain in battle.

13 And when Carden came on board the ship of Columbia, he bowed his head, and offered to put his sword, of curious workmanship, into the hands of Decatur.

14 But Decatur said unto him, Nay, thou hast defended thy ship like a valiant man; therefore, keep thy sword, but receive my hand.

15 So they sat down aud drank wine together; for the spirits of brave men mingle even in the time of warfare.

16 And after they had eaten and drank, Carden opened his mouth, for he was troubled iu his mind, and spake unto Decatur, saying:

17 Lo! if this thing which hath happened be known unto the king, that one of the vessels of Britain hath struck her flag, and become captive to a vessel of the United States, what shall be done unto the captain

thereof? for such a thing hath not been heard of among the nations of the earth.

18 And Decatur answered, and spake unto Carden, saying, Verily thou art deceived, neither will harm happen unto thee.

19 For, lo! it came to pass, about three score days ago, that one of the strong ships of the king, thy master, the name whereof was called Guerriere, fell an easy prey to one of the strong ships of Columbia; and they burnt her with fire upon the waters.

20 Now when Carden heard these words, his heart leaped with joy; for he dreaded the frowns of the king, and he was glad that he stood not alone in the thing.

21 After this, in the eighteen hundred and thirteenth year of the christian era, on the first day of the first month of the same year, and on the sixth day of the week,

22 The ship United States, and the ship Macedonian came into the haven of New-York, having passed a certain dangerous place called Hell-gate; and there was a heavy fog that day.

23 And there were great rejoicings in the city of New-York, and throughout the land of Columbia.

24 Moreover, there was a sumptuous dinner given to Isaac, Decatur, and Jones, in honor of their valiant deeds; and the number of the guests were about five hundred.

25 And the inhabitants of New-York made a great feast, on the ninth day of the month, for the brave mariners that wrought in the ship of Columbia.

26 And they became merry with the drinking of

wine ; after which they departed and went into a house
of mirth and gaiety.*

27 Now, it is written in the words of Solomon, whose
wisdom hath not been excelled, that, there is a time to
weep, and a time to rejoice.

28 Not many days after those things, it came to
pass, that the hearts of the lords and the counsellors of
Britain were rejoiced.

29 For a certain mighty ship, called the Southampton, fell upon a smaller vessel of the United States,†
and made capture thereof unto the king.

30 But the storm arose, and the sea beat upon the
vessels, and they were cast away, and they parted asunder, upon an island which lieth far to the south, and both
vessels were lost.

----

* *Theatre.*

† *United States' brig, Vixen, 12 guns, G. W. Reed,
commander.*

CHAP. XIV.

Affairs in the north—skirmishes—battle of Frenchtown, on the river Raisin—capture of Gen. Winchester's army—massacre of American prisoners.

———

Now it came to pass, that the wickedness of Britain had roused up the spirit of Satan in the savages of the forest, in the north and in the west.

2 And the tomahawk and the scalping knife were raised against the people of Columbia on the borders of the great lakes.

3 So the people sought after a valiant man to go against the savages and the men of Britain.

4 And they pitched upon a certain governor of one of the states in the west, whose name was Harrison,* and the great Sanhedrim made him a chief captain of the army.

5 Moreover, he was beloved by the people, and a mighty host of husbandmen were ready to follow after him.

6 And Harrison rested his army at the strong hold of Meigs, nigh the Miami Rapids, which lieth in the way journeying towards the strong hold of Malden, which is in the province of the king; whither he intended to go forth in the pleasant season of the year.

———

* *Maj. Gen. W. H. Harrison, Governor of Ohio,*

7 And Winchester* was another chief captain that went against the savages.

8 Now the savages had been a sore thorn in the side of the people of Columbia.

9 They had assailed the hold which is called after a chief captain, whose name was Dearborn, and their numbers overpowered it, and they used deceit, and put to death the men, and the women, and the infants that were found in the hold, after they had become captives, save about half a score.

10 And their howlings along the dark forest were more terrible than the wild wolf, and their murderous cunning more dreadful than the prowling tyger.

11 And the servants of the king gave them to drink of the strong waters of Jamaica, well knowing that they loved it as they did their own souls.

12 These were the allies, the messmates, the companions of the soldiers of Britain! hired assassins.

13 However, about this time there were many brave captains of the people of the United States that went against them.

14 Even Russel, and Hopkins, and Tupper, and Campbell, and Williams, and others, who drove the red savages before them,

15 And burnt their villages,* and laid waste their habitations, and slew many of them; for it is written in the holy scripture, Blood for blood!

16 Nevertheless, they treated the savage prisoners who fell into their hands kindly; neither suffered they the people to buffet them!

17 But it came to pass, on the twenty-second day of

---

* *Brig. Gen. Winchester.*

the first month, that a mighty horde of savages, and servants of the king, fell upon the army of Winchester the
chief captain.

18 And it was about the dawning of the day, when
the destructive engines opened their fires.

19 And the place where the battle was fought was
called, in the vernacular tongue, Frenchtown, which
lieth on the south side of the River Raisin, nigh unto
Lake Erie.

20 Now the name of the chief captain of the army
of Britain was Proctor, and he proved himself a wicked
man, and his name is despised even unto this day.

21 And when the battle waxed hot, and they began to
rush one upon another with great violence,

22 The small band of Columbia fought desperately,
and the slaughter was dreadful: and the pure snow of
heaven was sprinkled and stained with the blood of
men!

23 Nevertheless, the people of the United States
were overcome, and their chief captain made prisoner.

24 So when Winchester found he was made captive,
and that there was no hope for the rest of the men under
his command, he made a league with Proctor, the chief
captain of the host of the king.

25 In the which Proctor agreed to vouchsafe protection to the captive men of Columbia, from the wrath of
the savages, whom he had inflamed.

26 Now the number of the men of Columbia that
fell into their hands that day, were about five hundred;
and the slain and wounded about an hundred two score
and ten.

27 And the number of the savages and the men of Britain who fell in battle that day were many.

28 And Proctor removed the captives unto the strong hold of Malden, which lieth upon the opposite side of the river, iu the province of the king.

29 But, in the cruelty of his heart, he left the sick, the wounded, and the dying to the mercy of the savages of the wilderness !

30 In 'this thing he transgressed the word he had pledged, which is evil in the sight of the Lord.

31 Oh ! for a veil to hide in utter darkness the horrid deeds of that awful day, that they might not be handed down to the children of men, in the times to come.

32 Lo ! early in the morning of the next day, ere the sun had risen, the work of death began !

33 Behold the sullen savage, with deadly rage, drag forth the shivering soldier over the blood-stained snow fainting, bleeding with his wounds, and imploring on his knees for mercy.

34 Alas ! the savage understandeth not his words; but giveth him a blow with the hatchet of death.

35 For have not the counsellors of Britain said, For this will we give unto you silver and gold ?

36 Thus were the poor wounded prisoners of Columbia slaughtered in abundance.

37 And Round-Head, the chief captain of the warriors, and the savages under him, gat great praise from Proctor, the chief captain of the host of Britain.*

38 Neither did the sick and wounded escape, who

---

* *See Proctor's account, dated Quebec, Feb. 8, 1813.*

had gathered themselves together in the houses, that they might be sheltered from the piercing cold; even those who were weary and unable to go forth.

39 For the savages put the burning brand to the houses, from which they could not flee, and burnt them to death therein.

40 And the flames and the smoke arose; and their cries and their groans reached the high chancery of heaven,

41 Where they will stand recorded, until the coming of that day for which all other days were made.

42 Lo! these were the helpmates of the mighty kingdom of Britain, that noble and generous nation, the *bulwark of religion!*

43 Tell it not in Gath; publish it not in the streets of Askelon.*

----

* *The whole of this massacre was conducted under the eyes of the British officers, and sanctioned by them as well as by their government; this fact has never been disavowed.*

CHAP. XV.

Capture of the British frigate Java, by the United States frigate Constitution.

IN the twelfth month of the first year of the decree of the great Sanhedrim, on the twenty and ninth day of the month,

2 It came to pass, that one of the strong ships of the king had approached the country of the south, which lieth many thousand miles off.

3 And the ship was called Java, after one of the sweet scented islands of the east; where the poppy flourishes, where the heat of the sun is abundant, and where the Bohon Upas emits its deadly poison.

4 Moreover, she carried about four hundred and fifty men, and a governor;* and many officers and soldiers of the king; and she was well prepared for battle.

5 And Lambert commanded the ship of Britain, and he was a brave and valiant man.

6 So, as he passed along, nigh unto the coast of Brazil, where the sun casteth the shadow of a man to the south at noon day :

7 (A place unknown to the children of Israel, in the days of Moses)

8 Lo! one of the tall ships of Columbia, even the Constitution, beheld her when she was yet a great

---

* *Gov. Hyslop, and suite, bound to Bombay.*

way off, and made signs unto her which she answered
not ;

9 Which caused the gallant captain, whose sir-name
was Bainbridge,* to cast a shot towards her, after
which she received the thunder of his destroying engines.

10 And it was about the second hour after the mid-
day, when the sound of the battle-drum was heard.

11 And, as they approached towards each other, the
people shouted aloud, and the roaring of the engines was
dreadful.

12 And the servants of the king fought bravely; and
they held out to the last.

13 For they were ashamed to let the nations of the
earth say unto them,

14 Lo ! ye, who are the lords and the masters of the
mighty deep, have suffered these feeble Yankees to conquer you.

15 Therefore, the slaughter was dreadful, beyond
measure.

16 And the black clouds of smoke arose, and obscured the rays of the sun, so that they fought in the
shade.

17 And the winds moved the vessels about, and they
strove to avoid the balls of lead, and the heavy balls of
iron, that whistled about them in multitudes.

18 (Now these balls, which were gathered from the
bowels of the earth, were an invention unknown to
the Philistines ; even Sampson was a stranger to
them.)

-----

* *Com. Bainbridge.*

19 However, the ships fought hard, for the space of about two hours, when their thunders ceased.

20 And the ship of Britain had become a wreck, and the deck thereof was covered with blood!

21 Nevertheless, the servants of the king struck not the flag of Britain: for they were loth and hesitated:

22 But when Bainbridge, who saw this, came down upon them a second time, they humbled themselves, and drew down the British cross.

23 And the slain and the wounded of the king, that day, were an hundred three score and ten;

24 And those of the people of Columbia, were about thirty and four.

25 Moreover, Bainbridge, the captain of the vessel of the United States, was sorely wounded.

26 And Lambert, the captain of the ship of the king, was wounded, even unto death.

27 Now when the servants of the king were taken from the wreck, and meat and drink sat before them, that they might be refreshed, they partook thereof and were thankful.

28 And on the second day Bainbridge put a match to the black dust that remained in the ship, and she burst asunder, and rent the air with a loud noise.

29 And the fragments thereof were spread upon the waters round about.

30 And the fish of the sea, even the mighty whales, fled from the noise of the explosion.

31 However, the Constitution escaped not unhurt, for she was much wounded in her tackling.

32 So, when Bainbridge came into the haven of St. Salvador, which lieth farther to the south, he gave the

men of Britain, whom he had made captive, liberty to go home to the king, their master.

33 But when the tidings thereof reached the palace of the king, the lords and the princes and the rulers of Britain were confounded.

34 Their spirits sunk within them: astonishment seized the tyrants of the ocean.

35 The smile of joy had ..eparted from their countenances, and the gloom of despair hovered around them.

36 The wise men and the orators were mute; they gaped one upon another, and wist not what to say.

37 But the people of Columbia, from the north to the south, were gladdened; and bestowed great honor and praise on Bainbridge the captain.

38 Even the great Sanhedrim of the people rejoiced with great joy.

CHAP. XVI.

Com. Rodgers' return from a second cruise—capture of the U. States brig Viper—the General Armstrong and a British frigate—privateering.

Now it came to pass, in the beginning of the one thousand eight hundred and thirteenth year of the Great Founder of the Christian sect,

2 That a strong ship of the United States, called the President, commanded by Rodgers, returned a second time to the land of Columbia.

3 And while she was upon the waters of the great deep, she fell in with one of the packets of the king called after the swift flying bird* of the air, and made capture thereof.

4 And in the ship Rodgers found abundance of wealth, even an hundred, sixty and eight thousand pieces of silver.

5 And it was carried, with many horses, to a place of safe-keeping,† in the town of Boston, which lieth to the east.

6 Moreover, he made capture of another ship of the king,‡ laden with oil and bones of the great fish of the deep.

7 Now it happened, on the seventeenth day of the first month of the same year,

---

* *Swallow.* † *Bank of Boston.* ‡ *Ship Argo.*

8 That one of the weak vessels of the United States*
became a prey to one of the strong ships of the king,
called the Narcissus : albeit, she fought not.

9 About this time the great waters of the Chesapeake, which empty into the sea, were guarded by the
strong ships of the king, so that the vessels might not arrive or depart therefrom.

10 But the vessels of the United States, and the
private vessels of the men of Columbia, were doing
great damage unto the commerce of Britain, even in her
own waters.

11 And the number of the private vessels, that moved
swiftly over the face of the waters, and went out to de-
spoil the commerce of Britain, and to capture the merchant vessels thereof, was about two hundred two score
and ten.

12 And they made capture of more than fifteen hundred of the vessels of the people of Britain.†

13 Moreover, there was a sore battle between one
of the private armed vessels of the people of the United
States, and a strong ship of the king.‡

14 The privateer was called the General Armstrong,
and the name of the captain was Guy.||

15 Now Guy was a valiant man, and fear was a
stranger to him.

16 And on the eleventh day of the third month he
espied from afar a vessel which appeared as a speck
upon the waters.

17 But when he bore down upon her, behold! she

---

* Viper.   † During the war.   ‡ A British frigate.
|| Capt. Champlain.

F

was a fighting ship of Britain, carrying the destroying engines.

18 And Guy was near being entrapped, for he was deceived, thinking it was a merchant's vessel.

19 Therefore he was compelled to fight ; so he opened upon the vessel of the king, one of his mischievous engines called, in the vernacular tongue, Long-Tom.

20 And they fought hard, and the noise of the engines was very great.

21 And the balls of lead and iron showered around like hail-stones ; for the strong ship of Britain had them in abundance.

22 Now the slaughter was dreadful on both sides, and Guy was on the point of making capture of the ship : but he received a wound, and his vessel was disabled, so he made good his escape.

23 And the slain and the wounded of Guy were twenty and three, and the vessel of the king lost about twice that number.

24 Now, for this valiant act, Guy gat great honor, and the people give him a sword of fine workmanship.

25 Moreover, the Saratoga, the Scourge, the Chasseur, and many other private vessels of the people of the United States, were a grievous plague to the servants of the king ;

26 Inasmuch as some of them made sport with the mighty blockade of Britain, which she put forth against the free people of the land of Columbia.

27 For when they came nigh unto the coast of Britain, they made capture and burnt the vessels of the king, that carried rich merchandise, costly jewels, and silver and gold.

28 Yea, even in their own waters, and in the sight of their own havens, did they do these things.

29 For it happened that the cunning Yankees knew how to construct the swift-sailing vessels, that they outran the strong vessels of Britain.

30 And as the ships of Britain moved but slowly on the waters, so they caught them not.

31 Wherefore the artificers, the mechanics, and those who dealt in merchandise, raised their voices to the great council of Britain, saying,

32 Lo! are we not the faithful servants of the king, our master? have we not given unto him the one half of our whole substance? and shall these Yankees take from us the remainder?

33 Hath not the king a thousand ships of war? and wherefore should we be hemmed in?

34 Lo! our merchant vessels are idle! neither can we pass in safety even unto the land of Hibernia, which lieth nigh unto us.

35 And, behold, the captain of a private armed vessel of the Yankees, in derision of the proclamat on of our lord the king, hath proclaimed the island of Great Britain and her dependencies in a state of rigourous blockade; saying, Lo! I have the power to hem ye in.

36 Therefore, let the counsellors of the king ponder these things, and let the strong ships of Britain drive the vessels of Columbia from our coast.

37 Now the wisemen of Britain heard those things with sorrow; and they spake one to another concerning the matter:

38 But they wist not what to do; for the cunning of the captains of the fast sailing vessels of Columbia, surpassed the wisdom of the lords of Britain.

CHAP. XVII.

Capture and burning of Ogdensburgh by the British.

———

IN these days the war against Columbia was waged with great violence,

2 And the fur-clad savages prowled in secret places and fell upon the helpless.

3 ' They hid themselves in the wilderness; they couched down as a lion; and, as a young lion, they watched for their prey.'

4 The tall and leafless trees of the forest bent to the strong winds of the north; and the sound thereof was as the roaring of mighty waters.

5 Moreover, the face of the earth was covered with snow, and the water of the rivers was frozen.

6 And the borders of Columbia, nigh unto the province of the king, were exposed to the transgressions of the enemy.

7 And the soldiers of the king came in abundance from the island of Britain, and pitched their tents in the Canadian provinces.

8 Accordingly, it came to pass, on the twenty-second day of the second month, being the birth-day of Washington, the deliverer,

9 That a mighty host came out of the province of the king, and went against the town of Ogdensburgh, and made capture thereof.

10 And there were five slain and ten wounded of the people of Columbia, and about three score were taken by the servants of the king.

11 Moreover, the men of Britain gat much spoil; even a large quantity of the black dust fell into their hands;

12 And twelve of the destroying engines, which the people of Columbia had taken from the king about forty years before.

13 Also, three hundred tents, and more than a thousand weapons of war; but the vessels and the boats they consumed with fire.

14 Now Ogdensburgh was a beautiful village to behold; nevertheless they burned it with fire, and it became a heap of ruins.

15 And the women and the children looked for their homes, but found them not; and they sat down in sorrow, for the haughty conquerors laughed at their sufferings.

16 After which they returned with their spoil to Prescott, from whence they came, being on the other side of the water, in the province of the king.

17 And the honor that was given to the servants of Britain that day was as a thimble full of water spilt into the sea : for they were like unto a giant going out against a bulrush.

CHAP. XVIII.

*Capture of the Peacock, of 18 guns, by the U. S.
sloop of war Hornet, of 16 guns—return of the
Chesapeake from a cruise.*

———

THE deeds of the renowned warriors, the patriots,
and the valiant men of Columbia, have prepared a path
for the scribe, which he is compelled to follow :

2 But, as the soaring eagle moves to its craggy nest,
or the cooing dove to its tender mate, so is the compulsion
of his heart.

3 If the wickedness of Britain hath made manifest
her folly: if her sons have sat down in sackcloth and
ashes, the scribe looketh down upon her with pity.

4 It is written that, He who prideth himself in his
strength shall be humbled; and the haughty shall be
brought low.

5 And, if the Lord hath smiled upon the arms of
Columbia, let no man frown.

6 Now it came to pass, in the eighteen hundred and
thirteenth year of the christian era, on the twenty-fourth
day of the second month,

7 That one of the fighting vessels of Columbia, called
the Hornet, which signifieth, in the vernacular tongue,
a fly whose sting is poison,

8 Moved upon the waters of the great deep, far to
the south, near unto a place which is called Demarara.

9 Moreover, the captain of the Hornet was a valiant man, and his name was Lawrence.

10 And it was towards the setting of the sun, when he came nigh unto one of the strong ships of the king, called the Peacock, after the bird whose feathers are beautiful to behold;

11 And the captain thereof was sir-named Peake.

12 Now began the roaring noises of the engines of destruction, that opened their mouths against one another; and dreadful was the slaughter of that day.

13 Nevertheless, in the space of about the fourth part of an hour, the vessel of the king was captured by the people of Columbia.

14 And they found therein some of the mariners of the United States, who had begged that they might go down into the hold of the ship, and not raise their hands against the blood of their own brethren:

15 But Peake, the commander, suffered them not, but compelled them to fight against their own kinsmen: and one of them was slain in battle.

16 And the killed and maimed of the people of Britain, were about two score and two: and Peake the captain, was also slain: and the loss of Columbia was about five souls!

17 Moreover, the Peacock sunk down into the yawning deep, before they could get all the men of Britain out of her; and three of the people of Columbia were buried with her, whilst in the humane act of endeavouring to preserve the lives of the enemy,

18 Now this was the fifth fighting vessel of the king which had been humbled, since the decree of the great Sanhedrim, before the destroying engines of the people of Columbia.

19 And Lawrence, and the brave men that fought with him, had honor and praise poured out upon them abundantly.

20 Moreover, the people of New-York gave unto Lawrence vessels of silver, with curious devices; and they made a feast for the men who fought in the Hornet.

21 And all the people were exceedingly rejoiced at the valiant acts of Lawrence, and his fame extended throughout the land of Columbia; the sound of his name was the joy of every heart.

22 But when the news thereof reached the ears of the wise men of Britain, they said, Lo! these men are giants; neither are they like unto the warriors of the king.

23 And their witchcraft and their cunning are darkness unto us; even as when a man putteth a candle under a bushel.

24 Behold! five times hath the ' striped bunting' of Columbia, triumphed over the royal cross of Britain.

25 Now the great Sanhedrim, who were assembled together, forgat not the valiant deeds of the mariners of Columbia.

26 For they divided amongst them more than seventy thousand pieces of silver.

27 And it came to pass, on the tenth day of the fourth month, in the same year, that the Chesapeake, a strong vessel of the United States, arrived in the haven of Boston.

28 She had sailed upon the face of the rough wa-

ters more than an hundred days, after she departed from the land of Columbia, and passed a great way to the south :

29 And went hard by the island of Barbadoes, and those places, in the great sea which encompasseth the world, from whence they bring poisoned waters, which open the womb of the earth to receive the unwary sons of men.

30 Moreover, in returning, she came nigh unto the Capes of Virginia, where the sweet-scented plant* groweth in abundance.

31 And while she was on the ocean she captured a number of the vessels of the people of Britain, which were laden with rich merchandise.

* Tobacco.

CHAP. XIX.

*Capture of little York, in Upper Canada—the destruc-
tion of the whole American army prevented by the
precaution of Gen. Pike—his death.*

NOW, whilst these things happened in the south,
and the evils of war destroyed the life of man, and the
smiles of heaven strengthened the arms, and lifted up
the glory of Columbia.;

2 Behold, preparations of warfare were making on
the borders of the great lakes of the north.

3 And the vessels of war of Columbia that were upon the waters of the lake called Ontario, were commanded by a brave man, whose name was Chauncey.

4 Now on the twenty-fifth day of the fourth month,
the army of Columbia, who were gathered on the shore
of the lake, went down into the strong vessels of Chauncey.

5 And the number that went into the vessels was
about two thousand.

6 And Henry* and Zebulon, whose sir-name was
Pike,† were the chief captains of the host of Columbia.

7 On the same day the sails of the vessels were
spread to the winds of heaven, and they moved towards

** Major General Dearborn.   † Brig. Gen. Pike.*

a place called Little York,* in the province of Canada.

8 Howbeit, the winds were adverse and blew with great violence from the east.

9 Nevertheless, on the morning of the twenty-seventh day of the same mouth, the army of Columbia, commanded by Pike, the chief captain, moved out of the strong ships of the United States.

10 But Henry remained on board the vessel of Chauncey, neither came he to the water's edge.

11 And the place where the host of Columbia landed was to the west of the town, about twenty and four furlongs, and from the strong hold of the king about ten furlongs.

12 The gallant Forsyth, who led a band of brave men, who fought not for filthy lucre's sake, went before the host.

13 And their weapons of war were of curious workmanship, and they sent forth balls of lead; such as were unknown to Pharoah when he followed the Children of Israel down into the red sea.

14 Now Zebulon, with a thousand chosen men, followed close after Forsyth, the warrior.

15 About this time the savages and the servants of the king, even a great multitude, opened their engines of destruction without mercy.

16 And from the forest, and the secret places, their balls were showered like unto hail-stones, and the sound thereof was as sharp thunder.

17 And a man, whose name was Sheaffe, was the chief captain of the host of Britain.

---

* Capital of U. Canada.   † Rifles:

18 Now the destroying engines of the strong hold of the king issued fire and smoke with a mighty noise and shot at the vessels of the United States.

19 But Chauncey returned unto them four-fold; and and the battle waxed hot, both on the land and on the water.

20 And the men of Columbia rushed forward with fierceness, and drove the men of Britain from their strong hold.

21 So they fled towards the town for safety, for they were overcome; and the savages were smitten with fear, their loud yellings ceased, and their feet were light as the wild roe;

22 Nevertheless, the men of Columbia shouted aloud, and sounded their trumpets, their cymbals, and their noisy drums, which were contrived since the days of Jeroboam, king of Israel.

23 And Zebulon, the valiant warrior, followed hard after them; and they found no rest; for they were sore pushed, and the phantom of their imaginations pictured out new evils.

24 So when they found they were nigh being made captive, they departed in haste from the town and from the strong hold thereof, save about two score.

25 Now when the army of Britain was overthrown; when they were compelled to flee from the strong hold; the wickedness of Satan entered into their hearts.

26 And they gathered together abundance of the black dust and fixed it in the lowermost part of the fort, below the walls of stone.

27 After which they put a lighted match nigh to it,

so that when the whole army of Columbia got into the
hold, they might be destroyed.

28 But the Lord, who is good, even he who govern-
eth the destinies of man, permitted it not.

29 Now when Zebulon and his army came out of
the thick woods, in battle array, to go forth against the
strong hold,

30 Lo! they saw not the host of Britain; but the
eye of Zebulon was as the eye of an eagle, his strength
as the lion, and his judgment as the wise:

31 So he stayed his men of war from rushing forward towards the place, lest they might be entrapped:
and he caused them to move along the wood to the
right hand and to the left.

32 About this time, a stripling from the south, with
his weapon of war in his hand, ran up to Zebulon, and
spake unto him, saying,

33 Behold! a man of Britain appeareth in the fort;
suffer me, I pray thee, to slay him, for he is busied with
the destroying engines:

34 But Zebulon said, nay; we are yet a great way
off.

35 And the young man entreated him a second time,
saying, I beseech thee, let me step out before the host
and slay him, lest the engine be let loose upon us; then
Zebulon said unto him, Go.

36 So he ran out before the army and shot the man,
and he fell to the earth; and it was about a furlong off,
and the weight of the ball was about the weight of a
shekel.

37 But as the young man returned to where the army stayed, behold! the black dust in the hold caught

fire, and it rent the air with the noise of a thousand
thunders :

38 And the whole army fell down upon their faces*
to the earth ; and the stones, and the fragments of rocks,
were lifted high ; and the falling thereof was terrible
even unto death.

39 Yea, it was dreadful as the mighty earthquake,
which overturneth cities.

40 And the whole face of the earth round about, and
the army of Zebulon, were overshadowed with black
smoke ; so that, for a time, one man saw not another :

41 But when the heavy clouds of smoke passed away
towards the west, behold the earth was covered with the
killed and the wounded.

42 las ! the sight was shocking to behold ; as the
deed was ignoble.

43 About two hundred men rose not : the stones had
bruised them ; the sharp rocks had fallen upon them :.

44 They were wedged into the earth : their weapons
of war were bent down into the ground with them ;
their feet were turned towards heaven ; their limbs were
lopped off.

45 but when those who escaped unhurt arose and
looked around, they beheld not their chieftain; he had
fallen to the earth.

46 A huge stone smote him upon the back, and
two of his officers, (one of whom was the gallant

Fraser,) raised him up and led him forth from the field
of murder; the one on the one side, and the other on
the other side.

47 And as they led him away he turned his head
around to his brave warriors, and said unto them, Go
on; I will be with you soon! I am not slain.

48 The magic of his words gave joy to their hearts;
for they loved him as they loved their own father.

49 And with resistless force his noble band rushed on,
at the trumpet's sound, over the heaps of slain and
wounded, to glory, and to triumph!

50 And a swift messenger ran down unto Henry,
with these words in his mouth, Lo! the right hand of
our army is slain! its pride is gone! Zebulon has fallen?

51 Immediately Henry departed from the fleet, and
came to the shore, and went up and led the host of Columbia to the town and took it.

52 Now the slain, the maimed and the captives of
the host of Britain that day, were about a thousand
fighting men:

53 And the loss of the men of Columbia was about
three hundred slain and wounded.

54 And Henry, the chief captain, gave great honor to
the captains under him, even Riplev, Forsyth and Eus-
tis, and all the brave men that fought that day.

55 Nevertheless, Sheaffe, the captain of the king,
escaped with a handful of men, and the swift-footed
savages: leaving behind him the insignia of British
mercy!—a human scalp!

56 But the rejoicings of the people were mingled with deep sorrow; for the brave were slain in battle.

57 Oh! earth, how long shall thy inhabitants delight in warfare? when shall the old men cease to weep for their children?

58 Behold yon lonely widows; they weep for their husbands and their children; but they shall see their faces no more!

59 The fair daughters of Columbia sigh for the return of their beloved.

60 Seest thou those little ones? they fly to their disconsolate mother, they leap with joy at the name of father! but he shall never return!

61 Oh! that they had cast the black dust into the sea! t'en might not the children of men weep and wail.

62 Now on the next day, when the army of Zebulon gat the tidings that their captain was slain, the tears started in their eyes; they were mute, their hearts failed them; and they became as weak women.

63 Moreover, the United States made great lamentations over him; and the remembrance of his name shall live in the hearts of the people.

64 The eagle of Columbia dropt a feather from her wing, which the angel of brightness caught ere it fell to the earth, ascended to heaven, and recorded the name of PIKE.

CHAP. XX.

Sketches of the History of America.

———

THE the voice of many years shall drop upon the children of men ; and our children's children shall hearken unto it in the days to come.

2 The country of Columbia is a wide extended land, which reacheth from the north to the south, more than eight thousand miles ; and the breadth thereof is about three thousand.

3 Moreover the name of the country was called after the name of a great man, who was born in a place called Genoa ; being in Italia, on the sea-coast.

4 His name was Christopher, sir-named Columbus.

5 As the righteous man struggleth against wickedness, so did he against ignorance and stupidity.

6 Nevertheless, it came to pass, in the fourteen hundred and ninety second year of the Christian era, that he crossed the waters of the mighty deep, a thing that had never been known among the sons of men.

7 And the place where he landed was an island in the sea, nigh unto the continent of Columbia, called San Salvador ; which, being interpreted, signifieth a place of safety.

8 And the place was inhabited by wild savages, and they were naked.

9 Now when the people heard that Columbus had found a new land, they were astonished beyond measure,

for it was many thousand miles off; moreover, some of them strove to rob him of the honour, and he was treated wrongfully.

10 But his name was lifted up above his enemies, and it shall not be lost.

11 Now the land of Columbia is a most plentiful land, yielding gold and silver, and brass and iron abundantly.

12 Likewise, all manner of creatures which are used for food, and herbs and fruits of the earth:

13 From the red cherry, and the rosy peach of the north, to the lemon, and the golden orange of the south.

14 And from the small insect, that cheateth the microscopic eye, to the huge mammoth that once moved on the borders of the river Hudson; on the great river Ohio; and even down to the country of Patagonia in the south.

15 Now the heighth of a mammoth is about seven cubits and a half, and the length thereof fourteen cubits; and the bones thereof being weighed are more than thirty thousand shekels; and the length of the tusks is more than six cubits.

16 It is more wonderful than the elephant; and the history thereof, is it not recorded in the book of Jefferson, the scribe?*

17 The fierce tyger and the spotted leopard dwell in the dark forests; and the swift-footed deer upon the mountains and high places.

18 Now the number of inhabitants that are spread over the whole continent, is more than an hundred million.

------

* *Jefferson's notes on Virginia.*

19 And the people of Columbia, who are independent of the tyrants of the earth, and who dwell between the great river which is called Mississippi, in the south, and the province of Canada in the north, being numbered, are about ten thousand times ten thousand souls.*

20 The men are comely and noble, and cowardice hath forgot to light upon them : neither are they a superstitious people; they are peace-makers, they love the God of Israel, and worship him ; and there are no idolaters amongst them.

21 The women are passing beautiful ; they are like unto fresh lilies ; their cheeks are like wild roses ; their lips as a thread of-scarlet; nature hath gifted them with Roman virtue and patriotism ; and they have spread goodness with a plentiful hand.

22 Now it had happened in times past that the king of Britain had made war upon the people of Columbia, even forty years ago.

23 For the riches and prosperity of Columbia had become great, and the king coveted them.

24 And the war raged with the might of Britain, even in the heart of the land of Columbia, for about the space of seven years, when the army of Columbia became triumphant; neither could the power of Britain conquer the sons of liberty.

25 Accordingly a part of those who remained of the armies of Britain returned home to the king, their master; but a great number refused to return, prefer-

---

* The last census, in 1810, stated the amount at about 8,000,000, the number may now probably be increased to 10,000,000.

-ing a country whose mild laws are equally and righteous-ly dispensed, and where the hard earnings of industry are not taken away by the tax-gatherer:

26 So there was peace throughout the United States, and a covenant made between the nations.

27 But the names of the wise men of the great Sanhedrim in those days, and the names of those who fought hard in battle, and spilt their blood in the cause of liberty, are they not written in tne books of the chronicles of those days?

28 Now the fatness of the land of Columbia bringeth people from all nations to dwell therein.

29 The people of Columbia use no persuasion, the sacred cause of LIBERTY IS THE STAR OF ATTRACTION; and the time shall come when the eyes of all men shall be opened, and the earth shall rejoice.

30 Their laws are wholesome, for the people are the lawgivers, even as it was in the days of Cesar; but they know no kings.

CHAP. XXI.

Depredations in the Chesapeake—Havre-de-Grace burnt by the British under Adm. Cockburn—attack on Crany Island—Hampton taken by the British—outrages.

NOW it came to pass, that the mighty fleet of Britain, which was moving round about the great Bay of Chesapeake, committed much .evil upon the shores thereof.

2 And they robbed those who were defenceless, and carried away their fatted cattle, their sheep, and all those things which they found, and put them into the strong ships of the king.

3 Moreover, they burnt the dwellings of the helpless with fire, and they accounted it sport.

4 And the old men, the little children, and the women, yea, the fair daughters of Columbia, were compelled to fly from the wickedness of barbarians.

5 Even the small villages that rose beautifully on the river side, became a prey unto them, and were consumed by men who called themselves the mighty conquerors of Europe.

6 They were like hungry wolves that are never satisfied; destruction and devastation marked their footsteps

7 Now the ships of the king were commanded by a wicked man whose name was Cockburn.

8 And it was so, that on the third day of the fifth month, in the thirty and seventh year of the independence of the people of Columbia,

9 Cockburn, sir-named the wicked, led forth a host of the savage men of Britain, against a pleasant village, called Havre-de-Grace, which lieth on the borders of the Susquehanna, a noble river; being in the state of Maryland.

10 Now there was none to defend the place, save one man, whose sir-name was O'Neil, who came from the land of Hibernia, and him they made captive.

11 And they came as the barbarians of the wilderness: fierceness was in their looks, cruelty was in their hearts.

12 To the dwelling houses they put the burning brand, and plundered the poor and needy without pity; such wickedness was not done even among the Philistines.

13 The women and children cried aloud, and fell down at the feet of the chief captain of the king: but, alas! his heart was like unto the heart of Pharaoh; he heard them not.

14 However, it came to pass, the next day, when the pitiless Cockburn had collected his booty, and glutted his savage disposition, he departed.

15 And on the sixth day of the same month he went against other unprotected villages, which lie on the river Sassafras, called Frederickstown and Georgetown, and burnt them also.

16 So did he return to his wickedness as a dog returneth to his vomit.

17 Now about this time the number of the strong

ships of Britain was increased, and great multitudes of the soldiers of the king came with them to the waters of the Chesapeake.

18 And it came to pass, on the twenty-second day of the next month, that Cockburn, the chief captain of the ships of Britain, essayed to go against a small island, nigh unto Norfolk in the state of Virginia, called in the vernacular tongue, Crany-island.

19 And the number of the men of Britain that went against the island was about five thousand; and they began to get upon the shore at the dawning of the day.

20 Near unto this place a few vessels of Columbia, commanded by the gallant Cassin, were hemmed in by about a score of the mighty ships of the king.

21 Now the fighting vessels under Cassin were mostly small, and were called gun-boats, and they were little more than half a score in number.

22 Howbeit, but a few days before, they went against the Junon,* a strong ship of Britain, and compelled her to depart from before the mouths of the destroying engines.

23 But this island was defenceless; and there came to protect it an hundred brave seamen from the gun-boats, and an hundred and fifty valiant men from the Constellation, a fighting ship of the United States.

24 And they brought the destroying engines with them, and they let them loose upon the vessels of the king, and upon the men who were landing upon the shore.

British Frigate, Junon.

25 And the thundering noise thereof astonished the servants of the king: for they knew there was but a handful of men upon the island.

26 Moreover, Britain in her folly had introduced a new instrument of destruction, called Congreve Rockets, in honour of their inventor; and these were used in great abundance.

27 But they were harmless as turtle doves, for they killed not a man.

28 Now the men of Columbia, with their handicraft, shot the balls of iron strait as an arrow from a bow, and thereby did much damage to the servants of the king.

29 Inasmuch as they slew about two hundred of the men of Britain that day; and drove the host of them from the island.

30 So the mighty army of Britain fled in haste to the strong ships of the king for safety.

31 Now on the twenty-fifth day of the same month the army of Britain went against a village called Hampton, which lieth in the state of Virginia, and took it.

32 Howbeit, the little band of Columbia, commanded by Crutchfield, fought hard against them.

33 Nevertheless, they prevailed over him, and slew seven of his men, and wounded others, upon which he fled; for the men of Britain were like unto a swarm of locusts.

34 But the blood of two hundred royal invaders became a sacrifice to the wickedness of their leaders.

35 Oh! England! that a veil might be cast over thy transgressions of that day: but it cannot be.

36 Thy wickedness shall be written with a pen of iron, and with the point of a diamond.

37 It was here, even in Hampton, that thy strength and thy majesty rose up against the poor, the sick, and the needy.

38 Instead of protecting the tender women, the fairest work of God, the life of the world; behold! what hast thou done?

39 See! the shrieking matron cast herself into the waters that she may escape thy brutal violence : but all in vain; her garments are torn from her; she becomes a prey to thy savage lust.

40 Not she alone, but her daughter, and her fair sisters, have fallen into thy unhallowed hands, and been defiled !

41 Oh, Britain! the voice of violated chastity riseth up against thee; the mark of the beast is indelibly printed in thy forehead :

42 Even the old and weak men became victims of thy barbarity; thy servants stripped the aged Hope, and buffeted him; with the point of their swords did they torment him.

43 Do the groans of the murdered Kirby creep into thine ears ? go thou and repent of thine evil, and do so no more : the Lord God of Hosts shall be thy judge ;

44 The generous people of Columbia may possibly forgive thy crimes against them ; but the remembrance thereof shall live to the end of time ; neither shall they forget the name of Cockburn.

H

CHAP. XXII.

Russian mediation—Bayard and Gallatin sail for St. Petersburgh—the British compelled to abandon the siege of Fort Meigs.

———

THE lofty eagle cutteth the air with his wings, and moveth rapidly along; the fish of the deep glide swiftly through the waters; the timid deer bounds through the thick forests with wonderful speed:

2 But Imagination surpasseth them all; she rideth on the fleet winds; she holdeth a stream of lightning in her hand.

3 In an instant she flieth from the frozen mountains of Zembla, in the regions of the north, to the burning sands of Africa in the torrid zone.

4 Now the sons of Columbia were peace-makers; neither did their footsteps follow after warfare.

5 And, it is written in the holy scriptures, Blessed are the peace-makers, for they shall be called the children of God.

6 So the great Sanhedrim of the people sent two of the wise men of Columbia, the one named Gallatin and the other Bayard, into a distant country:

7 Even unto the extensive country of Russia, that there they might meet the wise men of Britain, and heal the wounds of the nations, and make peace with one another.

8 But the people of Britain yielded not to the entreaties of the great Sanhedrim; therefore the war continued to rage.

9 So it came to pass, on the fifth day of the fifth month, in the pleasant season of the year; when the trees put forth their leaves and the air is perfumed with the sweet scent of flowers, and the blue violets bespread the green hillocks;

10 That Harrison, the chief captain, from the west the brave warrior, who had entrenched himself in the strong hold of Meigs, nigh unto the river Miami, sallied forth against the savages and the men of Britain, that hemmed him in.

11 Now there were about a thousand soldiers of the king, and a thousand savages that had besieged the fort many days; and threw therein the balls of destruction, and strove to make captive the army of Columbia.

12 Nevertheless, Harrison, and his gallant little band, fought hard against them, and drove them from before the strong hold with great slaughter.

13 Likewise, the slain of Columbia was about four score, besides the wounded.

14 Moreover, the chief captain gave great honour to Miller and all the captains and soldiers under him; even those called militia.

15 And the names of the states of Ohio and Kentucky were raised high, by the valiant acts of their sons that day.

CHAP. XXIII.

Surrender of Fort George and Fort Erie to the Americans—Gen. Brown drives the British from before Sackett's Harbour with great loss—Gens. Winder and Chandler made prisoners at Forty-mile Creek.

NOW, on the twenty-seventh day of the same month, being thirty days after Zebulon had gone to sleep with his fathers,

2 Henry, whose sir-name was Dearborn, and Lewis,* the chief captains of the army of Columbia, and Chauncey the commander of the fleet of the United States, that moved on the waters of the great lake Ontario, essayed to go against Fort George and Fort Erie, in the province of the king

3 For they had previously concerted their plan and matured it ; and taken on board the ships, the army of Columbia, and a number of the destroying engines.

4 And when the vessels of Chauncey came nigh unto the place, they let the engines loose upon the fort, with a roaring noise.

5 In the meantime the army landed upon the shore, and went against the servants of the king.

---

* *Gen. Morgan Lewis.*

6 And the men of Britain were frightened at the sound of the warring instruments that reached their camp, and they fled in dismay towards the strong hold of Queenstown.

7 And they destroyed their tents, and their store-houses, and put a match to the black dust of their magazines, and blew them up into the air : this they did even from Chippewa to Albino.

8 Moreover, the slain and wounded of the king were two hundred two score and ten; of the men of Columbia about three score were slain and maimed.

9 So the forts of George and Erie were captured by the army and navy of the United States.

10 And Henry and Isaac, whose sir-name was Chauncey, spake well of all the captains and men that fought with them.

11 The gallant captains Scott and Forsyth fought bravely; neither were they afraid.

12 Boyd, and M'Comb, and Winder, and Chandler, and Porter, and a host of heroes, turned not aside from the heat of the battle.

13 And here the noble spirit of the youthful Perry burst forth into view; a man made to astonish the world, and shower down glory upon the arms of Columbia.

14 Now it happened about the same time, that the strong ships of Britain moved towards the other end of the lake, to the east thereof, and went against a place called Sackett's Harbor.

15 The fleet of the king was commanded by a chief captain whose name was Yeo; and Prevost, the governor of Canada, commanded the army.

16 And on the morning of the twenty-ninth day of the month, they landed more than a thousand men on the shores of Columbia.

17 Howbeit, a certain valiant man, even Jacob, whose sir-name was Brown, commanded the host of Columbia that went against them :

18 And Jacob, albeit a man of peace,* drove the men of Britain, and compelled them to flee rapidly from the shore, and get them into their vessels.

19 So Prevost and Yeo returned to the strong hold of Kingston.

20 And the skill of Jacob, in driving away the soldiers of the king, pleased the people, and they honoured him greatly.

21 Not many days after these things, there was a sore battle fought, near to a place called Forty-mile Creek.

22 And it was so that Winder and Chandler, two brave captains of the United States, and about four score men, were come upon unawares in the darkness of the night, and made captive by the servants of the king.

23 After which they were conveyed to the strong hold of Montreal, which lieth in the province of Canada, on the river St. Lawrence.

24 The officers and soldiers of Columbia fought bravely, and there were many slain and wounded on both sides :

25 Nevertheless, the army of the United States rested nigh unto the place.

———

* Gen. Brown is a Quaker.

CHAP. XXIV.

Capture of the Chesapeake—-Commodore Decatur blockaded in New-London.

IN these days the pride of Britain was sorely wounded: for she had been discomfited upon the waters of the great deep; and disappointment had sharpened her anger.

2 The people of Columbia had triumphed over her ships; and her mighty armies had gained no honors.

3 Notwithstanding she had made peace with the nations of Europe, and her whole strength was turned against the people of Columbia.

4 The prosperity of many hundred years had flattered her, and she was puffed up with the vanity thereof; yea, she had forgotten herself.

5 So it came to pass, on the first-day of the sixth month, that a certain strong ship of the king, called the Shannon, appeared before the haven of Boston, which lieth to the east.

6 And she bade defiance to the vessels of Columbia; for she had prepared herself for the event.

7 Now the Chesapeake, a fighting ship of the United States, was nigh unto the place; and she was commanded by the brave Lawrence, who had gained much honor in the sight of the people; neither was he afraid.

8 And he went forth to battle against the vessel of the king, which was commanded by Broke, a valiant man.

9 Moreover, the mischievous engines that were in the ship of Britain were more, and the number of their men greater than those of the vessel of the United States.

10 For Broke had gotten about two hundred men, and secreted them; so that when the hour of danger arrived they might assist his men, and fall unawares upon the men of Lawrence.

11 Nevertheless, towards the going down of the sun, the vessels drew nigh to each other.

12 And Lawrence spake unto his officers and his mariners, saying:

13 Now shall we set our engines at the work of destruction; let the fire issue out of their mouths, as it were like unto fiery dragons.

14 And although their numbers be greater than ours, yet we may be conquerors; for he who is little of spirit gaineth nothing.

15 But if, peradventure, we should be overcome, even then shall not the sacred cause of LIBERTY perish, neither shall the people of Columbia be disheartened.

16 Also, your names shall be recorded as the champions of freedom.

17 And the nations of the earth shall learn with astonishment, how dearly you prize the inheritance of your fathers.

18 Now when Lawrence had made an end of speaking, they sat the destroying engines to work, and rushed one upon another like fierce tygers.

19 The fire and smoke were abundant, and tremendous was the noise that rent the air and floated upon the waters.

20 And the Chesapeake fell close upon the Shannon, swords clashed with swords, and pikes with pikes; and dreadful was the conflict thereof.

21 But the men of Broke were more numerous than the men of Lawrence, and overpowered them, by the means of their numbers.

22 Already had the valiant Lawrence fallen; his life-blood flowed fast; still he cryed out to his brave companions, saying unto them, Don't give up the ship; his noble spirit fled, but his name shall not perish.

23 Moreover, about this time all the officers of the ship of the United States were either slain or sorely wounded; so she was captured by the vessel of the king.

24 And Satan rose up in the hearts of the conquerors, and they shot the balls of death down into the hold of the vessel of the United States, even against the halt and maimed who had surrendered themselves.

25 And when the tidings thereof reached the kingdom of Great Britain, the lords, the princes, the rulers, yea, all the people were rejoiced beyond measure.

26 And they bade their roaring engines utter their voices in London, their chief city, that had been silent many years, even those in the great tower,* which was built by William the Bastard, more than seven hundred years ago.

On this occasion they fired their tower guns, which had not been done since Nelson's victory.

27 Their joy was unbounded, for they had overcome one of the strong ships of Columbia.

28 Now the slain and the wounded on board the Chesapeake, were an hundred two score and four ; and there fell of the servants of the king about two hundred.

29 Amongst the slain of Columbia were also Augustus, whose sir-name was Ludlow, and another brave officer whose name was White.

30 And when the people of Columbia heard of a truth that Lawrence was slain, they mourned for him many days.

31 His body was conveyed to a place called Halifax, in the province of the king, where they honoured his memory, and buried him for a while.

32 But in a short time thereafter his body was taken out of the earth, with the body of Ludlow, and conveyed to the city of New-York, for interment.

33 And the captain's name who volunteered his services in this act of patriotism, and who brought the bodies away from Halifax, was Crowningshield, of Salem, in the state of Massachusetts.

34 So Lawrence was buried in the burial-place of his fathers, in his own land : and a great multitude of people went out to behold the funeral as it passed through the city.

35 And his valiant deeds shall live forever in the remembrance of the people.

36 About this time, on the fourth day of the month, the brave Decatur essayed to go forth with his vessel upon the waters of the mighty deep.

37 And the vessels that were with him were called

the United States, the Hornet, and the Macedonian; the latter a strong ship which he had captured from the king.

38 But it was so, that some large vessels of Britain, carrying each of them more than seventy of the destroying engines, suffered him not to go forth.

39 Moreover, they wished to retake the Macedonian, that they might retrieve the shame of the capture thereof.

40 So the ships of Britain blockaded Decatur and his ships in the haven of New-London, which lieth in the state of Connecticut, nigh unto a place called Stonington, and they remained there many months.

CHAP. XXV.

Capture of Col. Boerstler and Major Chapin with their command—treatment of Prisoners—Major Chapin's escape.

———

NOW there was much hard fighting on the borders, for the nations were wroth against one another, and many men were slain by the sword.

2 But it is written in the book of Jeremiah the prophet, that He who is slain by the sword, is better than he who is slain by famine.

3 Nevertheless, many of the soldiers of Columbia suffered hunger : for they had given unto them unwholesome food, and a scanty fare,

4 Although, when the servants of the king became captives to the people of Columbia, they were kindly treated, and partook of the fat of the land.

5 Now it came to pass, in the second year of the war, on the twenty third day of the sixth month,

6 That a captain of the United States, whose sirname was Boerstler, was ordered to go forth from the strong hold of Fort George, to annoy the enemy.

7 And the name of the place where he essayed to go, was called Beaver-dams, being distant from the strong hold of Queenstown about seventy furlongs.

8 And the number of the men of war of Columbia who followed' after him was little' more than five hundred.

9 But when they came nigh unto the place, early in the morning of the next day, lo! they were encompassed round about by the savages and soldiers of the king.

10 Nevertheless, they fought bravely for a time; and Dearborn, the chief captain of Fort George, sent the valiant Chrystie to help him out of his snare.

11 But Boerstler and his army had already become captive to the men of Britain.

12 And they made a covenant in writing, between one another, but the men of Britain violated the covenant.

13 Inasmuch as they permitted the savages to rob the officers of their swords, and their apparel, yea, even the shoes from off their feet.'

14 After which the men of Columbia were commanded to go, in boats, down to the strong hold of Kingston, in the province of the king.

15 But a certain brave captain, called Chapin,* a cunning man withal, made his escape in a boat, and arrived at the strong hold of Fort George; having, .by the strength of his single arm, overpowered three of the strong men of Britain.

---

* *Major Chapin.*

CHAP. XXVI.

*Capture of Fort Schlosser and Black Rock——Gen.
Dearborn resigns his command to Gen. Boyd, on
account of sickness——the Six Nations of Indians
declare war against Canada.*

———

AND it came to pass, on the fourth day of the seventh
month, which is the ·birth day of Columbian Liberty
and Independence,

2 In the dark and solemn hour of the night, when the
deadly savage walketh abroad, and the hungry wolves
howl along the forest,

3 A band of the men of Britain crossed over the
water from Chippawa to a place called Fort Schlosser,

4 And there was a handful of the men of the United
States in the place, whom they made captive, being
twelve in number.

5 Likewise, they carried away the bread and the
meat, and some of the strong waters; also one of the
destroying engines.

6 Moreover, the engine which they brought away was
made partly of brass, partly of iron, and partly of wood.

7 And the weight of the ball that issued out of its
mouth was about two hundred shekels, after the shekel
of the sanctuary.

8 On the tenth day of the same month they also passed over the river Niagara, towards a place called Black Rock, and the small band at the place fled.

9 And they destroyed the strong house, and the camp with fire, and carried away the flour, and the salt, and such things as they stood in need of.

10 However, while they were yet carrying them away, there came a band of men of the United States, from the village of Buffaloe,

11 And let their instruments of war loose upon them; and smote them even unto death; albeit, those who were not slain escaped with their plunder.

12 And they fled hastily away, leaving nine of their slain behind, and more than half a score of captives.

13 The soldiers of the king were commanded by two men, the one called Bishop and the other Warren, and the men of Columbia were commanded by a chief captain, named Porter.*

14 About this time the savages and the men of war of Britain assailed the guards and the out-posts near unto Fort George

15 Day after day and night after night did they annoy them; and many were slain on both sides.

16 And Dearborn, the chief captain of the fort, and of the host of Columbia round about Niagara, became sick and unable to go out to battle.

17 So Boyd, a brave and tried warrior, was made chief captain in his stead, until Wilkinson, the chief captain, arrived: and the gallant Fraser was appointed one of his aids.

---

* Gen. P. B. Porter.

18 Now there were some amongst the tribes of the savages, who had been instructed in the ways of God, and taught to walk in the path of righteousness;

19 For the chief governor of the land of Columbia, and the great Sanhedrim of the people, had taken them under their care.

20 And sent good men amongst them to preach the gospel, and instruct them in the sublime doctrine of the Saviour of the world.

21 And they hearkened unto the preachers, and were convinced, and their natures were softened.

22 Amongst these tribes were those who were called the Six nations of New York Indians;

23 And their eyes were opened, and they saw the evil and wickedness of Britain.

24 So their chiefs and their counsellors rose up and made war against the province of Canada, and fought against the hired savages of the king of Britain.

25 But in all their acts they suffered not the spirit of barbarians to rule over them.

26 They remembered the good counsel given to them by their aged chief.*

27 And when the red savages and the men of Britain fell into their hands, they raised neither the tomahawk nor the scalping knife.

28 Nay, they treated them kindly; and those who were slain in battle they disturbed not; and their humanity exceeded the humanity of the white men of Britain.

---

* *Alluding to an eloquent speech, delivered about that time, to the Six Nations, by one of their old warriors.*

CHAP. XXVII.

*Affairs on Lake Ontario, between the fleets of Com.
Chauncey and Sir James Yeo.*

IN those days, the great waters of the lake Ontario
were troubled with the movements of the fighting ships
of Columbia, as well as those of the king.

2 Now the fleet of the king, which was commanded
by Yeo, who was a skilful captain, was greater than the
fleet of Columbia, which was commanded by the brave
Chauncey.

3 And they had contrived to move to and fro upon the
bosom of the lake Ontario many months,

4 And two of the small vessels, called the Julia and
the Growler, being parted from the fleet, fell into the
hands of Yeo.

5 Nevertheless, Chauncey followed after Yeo, and
hemmed him in for a time.

6 But a strong west wind arose and the fleets were
again separated.

7 After this Chauncey captured a number of small
fighting vessels, and about three hundred soldiers of the
king.

8 Now it was so, that when Yeo put his fleet in battle
array, as though he would fight,

9 Then Chauncey went out against him, to meet him,
and give him battle ; but the heart of Yeo failed him
and he turned aside from the ships of Columbia.

10 So Chauncey sailed along the borders of the lake, from the one end to the other; even from Niagara to Sackett's Harbour, and Yeo followed him not.

11 Now all the vessels of the king, and all the vessels of the United States, that carried the destroying engines, upon the lake Ontario, being numbered were about seventeen.

12 Howsoever, they cut down the tall trees of the forest, and hewed them, and built many more strong vessels; although they had no gophar-wood amongst them in these days.

13 And they made stories to them, even to the third story, and they put windows in them, and they pitched them within and without with pitch; after the fashion of the ark.

14 And, lo! some of the ships which they built upon the lake, carried about an hundred of the engines of death.

15 And the weight of a ball which they vomited forth was about a thousand shekels.

16 Now the rest of the acts of Chauncey and Yeo, which they did, are they not written in the book of Palmer, the scribe?*

---

* *Historical Register, an excellent publication, in 4 vols. octavo, printed in Philadelphia, 1816, which contains the facts and the official documents of the late war.*

CHAP. XXVIII.

*Affairs on Lake Champlain—pillage of Plattsburgh by
the British—bombardment of Burlington—depredations committed in the Chesapeake, and along the coast.*

NOW the fighting vessels of Britain began to appear
upon the lake, called by the ancient Gauls, Champlain.

2 And the vessels of war of Columbia that were upon
the waters of the lake were not yet prepared for the
battle; the name of their commander was M'Donough,
a stripling.

3 So, it came to pass, on the thirty and first day of
the seventh month, that the vessels of the king came forward against Plattsburgh, which lieth on the borders of
the lake.

4 And there were none to defend the place; for the
army of Hampton, a chief captain of the United States,
was encamped upon the opposite side of the lake, at a
place called Burlington, in the state of Vermont.

5 And the number of the soldiers of the king that landed at Plattsburgh was more than a thousand men, and
the name of their chief captain was Murray.

6 And a captain of the United States, whose name
was Mooers, a man of valor, strove to gather together

the husbandmen of the place ; but they were not
enough.

7 So the army of the king captured the place; and
the men of Columbia fled before the men of Britain.

8 Moreover, the wickedness which had been committed at Hampton, was noised abroad, even from the
shores of Virginia to lake Champlain.

9 Accordingly, all the women and children, who
were able, suddenly departed from the place, lest the
same thing might, peradventure, happen unto them.

10 Neither were they deceived in judgment; for, lo!
when the place was given up, and a covenant made, the
servants of the king proved faithless.

11 They abided not by the contract; saying, Pish! ye
are but yankees, therefore will we do to you as seemeth
meet unto us !

12 So they burnt the houses, and all other things be-
longing to the United States, with fire.

13 After which they fell upon the merchandise, the
goods, and the chattles of all manner of persons; nay the
persons of some of the women were abused :

14 Meanwhile they forced others to put the burning
brand to their own dwellings; or pay them tribute.

15 They killed the cattle, and prepared them food ;
and after they had eaten and drank, they overturned
the tables.

16 So, when their vengeance was completed, they
departed to other places and committed like evils.

17 About the same time the vessels of the king that
sailed on the lake, went against the town of Burlington,
where the army of Hampton was.

18 But when the men of Columbia began to let the

destroying engines loose upon them, from the strong hold before the town, they fled in dismay.

19 Now while these things were passing in the north, the greedy sons of Britain were laying desolate the small villages of the south.

20 On the waters of the Chesapeake they captured the small vessels and made spoil thereof.

21 Moreover, they gat possesion of a small place called Kent Island, and robbed the poor and needy; for there was no mercy in them.

22 Yea, it was said of a truth, and talked abroad, that they came in the night time, and disturbed the small cattle, and the fowls, and took them for their own use, and crawled away like men ashamed;

23 Thus committing a sin, by violating the eighth commandment of God, which saith, THOU SHALT NOT STEAL.

24 Even the state of North-Carolina escaped them not; they landed a thousand men of war at a place called Ocracocke.

25 And again the work of destruction began; they spread terror and dismay whithersoever they went.

26 They troubled the men of Columbia all along the sea coast, which is more than eight thousand furlongs, from north to south.

27 Moreover, they gat much plunder; even much of the good things with which the land of Columbia aboundeth.

CHAP XXIX.

Major Croghan defeats the British and Indians, under Gen. Proctor, in their attack on Fort Stephenson, Lower Sandusky.

———

NEVERTHELESS, it came to pass, that Harison, the chief captain of the north west army, had placed a captain, a young man, in the hold called Fort Stephenson, to defend it.

2 Now the fort lieth at the western end of the great lake Erie, at a place called Sandusky.

3 And the number of the soldiers that were with the youth in the hold was about an hundred and three score, and they had only one of the destroying engines.

4 Now the name of the young man was George, and his sir-name was Croghan.

5 So, on the first day of the eighth month, about the going down of the sun, a mighty host from Malden appeared before the hold ;

6 Even a thousand savages, and about five hundred men of war of Britain ; and Proctor was the commander thereof.

7 Moreover, they brought the instruments of destruction in great plenty even howitzers, which were not known in the days of the children of Israel.

8 And they had prepared themselves for the fight,

and encompassed the place round about, both by land and by water.

9 After which Proctor sent a message to the brave Croghan, by a captain whose name was Elliot, and the words thereof were in this sort :

10 Lo ! now ye can neither move to the right nor to the left, to escape, for we have hemmed you in ;

11 Therefore, that your blood may not be spilt in vain, we command that ye give up the strong hold into the hands of the servants of the king, and become captives.

12 We have the destroying engines in abundance, and we are a numerous host.

13 Furthermore, if ye refuse then shall the wild savages be let loose upon you ; and there shall be none left among you to go and tell the tidings thereof.

14 But when Croghan heard the message, he answered and said unto Elliot, Get thee now to thy chief captain, and say unto him, I refuse ; neither will I hearken unto him :

15 And if it be so, that he come against me with his whole host, even then will I not turn aside from the fierce battle; though his numbers were as the sand on the sea shore.

16 Lo ! David, of old, with a sling and a stone, slew the mighty Goliah : and shall the people of Columbia be afraid, and bow before the tyrants of Europe ?

17 Then Elliot returned to the army of the king ; and immediately the mouths of their engines were opened against the fort.

18 And the noise thereof continued a long time ; even until the next day ; but their battering prevailed not.

19 Now when Proctor saw it was of no avail, he di-

vided his host into two bands, and appointed a captain to each band; and they moved towards the fort and assailed it with great violence.

20 But the men of Croghan were prepared for them; and they let loose their weapons of war upon them, and set their destroying engine to work, and smote the men of Britain, hip and thigh, with great slaughter.

21 And the deep ditch that surrounded the fort was strewed with their slain and their wounded.

22 So the host of Britain were dismayed and overthrown, and fled in confusion from the fort into the forest; from whence, in the dead of the night, they went into their vessels, and departed from the place.

23 Now the loss of the men of Britain was about an hundred two score and ten; and of the men of Columbia there was one slain and seven wounded.

24 But when Proctor had rested his army he sent a skilful physician to heal the maimed which he had fled from and left behind.

25 But Harison, the chief captain, said unto him, Already have my physicians bound up their wounds, and given them bread and wine, and comforted them; after the manner of our country.

26 For we suffer not the captives that fall into our hands to be buffeted or maltreated; neither want they for any thing.

27 So the physician of the king's army was permitted to return to his own camp.

28 Moreover, great honor and praise were bestowed upon the brave Croghan, the captain of the fort, for his valiant deeds; and his name was spoken of with joy throughout the land of Columbia.

CHAP. XXX.

*British schooner Dominica, of 14 Guns, captured by
the privateer Decatur, of 7 guns—U. S. brig Argus
captured by the Pelican—capture of the Boxer by
the U. S. brig Enterprize.*

NOW the war continued to rage without abatement
upon the waters of the great deep;

2 And manifold were the evils that came upon the
children of men by the means thereof.

3 Moreover, the great Sanhedrim of the people
were forced to bestir themselves; and they had continued their councils day after day without ceasing.

4 And it came to pass, that there was a dreadful
battle fought between a vessel of the king, and a private
vessel of Columbia.

5 And the name of the vessel that fought was Decatur, and the captain's name was Diron, a Gaul.

6 And it was so, that about the fourth day of the
eighth month, the Decatur having sailed out of the haven of Charleston, being in the state of South Carolina,
fell in with one of the fighting vessels of the king, called
the Dominica.

7 But the destroying engines of the king's vessel
were two fold greater in numbers than those of the
Decatur.

K

8 Nevertheless, they set them to work, so that they groaned beneath the fire and smoke;

9 And in about the space of an hour the Dominica was conquered and taken captive.

10 For when the vessels came close together, the men smote one another with their swords and weapons of war; yea, even the balls of iron they cast at each other, with their hands, and slew one another with wonderful slaughter.

11 Inasmuch as there were slain and maimed of the king three score souls; those of the Decatur were about a score : moreover the captain of the Dominica was slain.

12 The fight was an unequal one; and the bravery of Diron gained him a great name, for he overcame the enemies of freedom; although their force was greater than his.

13 After this, on the fourteenth day of the same month, there was another sore battle between a small vessel of the United States, called the Argus and the Pelican, a ship of the king.

14 Now the Pelican was somewhat stronger than the Argus, and they were stubborn and kept the destroying engines to work, with great noise about forty and five minutes.

15 And the brave captain of the Argus, whose name was Allen, was wounded unto death, and the vessel of Columbia was captured by the ship of Britain, the name of the commander whereof was Maples.

16 Of the men of Columbia six were slain and seventeen wounded; of the men of Britain the slain and wounded were five.

17 Now the death of Allen was spoken of with sorrow throughout the land of Columbia, for he had defended the vessel of the United States nobly ; and captured some merchant ships of Britain.

18 Even the enemy regarded him for his bravery, for they buried him with honour in their own country, not far from the place where he became captive, which was in the waters of the king, even in St. George's Channel.

19 But it came to pass, on the fifth day of the next month, in the same year,

20 That a certain small vessel of Columbia, carrying the engines of destruction, commanded by a gallant man, whose name was Burrows, fell in with another small vessel of the king, called the Boxer and the captain thereof was a brave man, and his name was Blythe.

21 In the language of the people of the land, the vessel of Columbia was called the Enterprize.

22 Now when the vessels drew nigh unto each other the men shouted with loud shouting.

23 And immediately they let the mischievous engines loose upon one another, with a noise like unto thunder.

24 But it happened, that in about the space of forty minutes, the Boxer was overcome ; but she was taken somewhat unawares :

25 For, lo ! the pride of the men of Britain had made them foolish : and, thinking of the conquest, they nailed Britannia's red-cross to the mast of the vessel.

26 Whereupon, after they were overcome, they cried aloud for mercy, saying,

27 Behold! our colors are fast; and we cannot quickly unloose them; nevertheless, we will be prisoners unto you, therefore spare us.

28 So the brave mariners of Columbia spared them, and stopped the destroying engines; for their hearts were inclined to mercy.

29 However, this was another bloody fight; for there fell of the men of Britain forty that were slain outright, and seventeen were wounded.

30 And the loss of Columbia in slain and maimed was about fourteen.

31 And the commanders of both vessels were slain; and they buried them with honor in the town of Portland, which leaveth Boston to the west; for the battle was fought hard by.

32 Moreover, the great Sanhedrim was pleased with the thing, and gave unto the nearest kinsman of Burrows a medal of gold, in token of remembrance thereof.*

** Mathew L. Davis, of New-York, a printer, a patriot, and a philantropist, on a tour in the eastern States, passing through Portland and the burial place of Burrows (which was without a memorial,) being pointed out to him, generously delayed his journey until, at his own expense, he had caused a monument to be erected over the grave of the valiant; which bears the following inscription, equally creditable to the modest merit of Mr. Davis,—to his head, and to his heart:*

CHAP. XXXI.

The capture of the British Fleet on Lake Erie, by the American Fleet, under Com. Perry.

———

THE Lord, in the plenitude of his wisdom and power, ordaineth all things which come to pass : and the doings are for the benefit of man, and for the glory of God.

2 For where is the evil which hath not turned to an advantage, and been a warning, and swallowed up the evil that might have come ?

———

BENEATH THIS STONE
Moulders
THE BODY OF
WILLIAM BURROWS,
Late Commander of the
UNITED STATES' BRIG ENTERPRIZE,
Who was mortally wounded on the 5th of September, 1813, in an action, which contributed to increase the fame of American valour, by capturing his
BRIT. MAJESTY'S BRIG BOXER,
after a severe contest of 45 minutes.
A passing stranger has erected this monument of respect to the manes of a patriot, who in the hour of peril, obeyed the loud summons of an injured country, and who gallantly met, fought and conquered the foeman.

3 Now about this time the strong vessels of Columbia that moved upon the face of the blue waters of the great lake Erie, were given in charge to Oliver, whose sirname was Perry.

4 And he was a prudent man, and had prepared himself to meet the vessels of the king, even forty days beforehand.

5 And the name, of of the captain of the fleet of Britain was Barclay, a man of great valor; but he boasted and was vain of his fleet, for it was more powerful than the fleet of Columbia.

6 Nevertheless, it came to pass, in the one thousand eight hundred and thirteenth year, on the tenth day of the ninth month, early in the morning, about the rising of the sun,

7 The valiant Perry beheld the fleet of the king at a distance upon the lake; so he unmoored his vessels and went out to meet them in battle array, fleet against fleet.

8 And when their white sails were spread upon the bosom of the lake, they appeared like unto a squadron of passing clouds.

9 A gentle breeze wafted the hostile vessels towards one another.

10 It was silence upon the waters; save when the sound of musical instruments fell sweetly upon the ear.

11 But it happened, a little before the mid-day, that the shouts of the men of war of Britain were heard, and the shouts of the men of Columbia.

12 And now the destroying engines began to utter

their thunders vomiting forth fire and smoke and brimstone in abundance.

13 And suddenly the waters were in an uproar; and
the bellowing noises sounded along the lake.

14 Moreover, the chief force of the ships of the king
was put against the vessel in which Perry was;

15 And the vessel was called the Lawrence, after a
brave man, whose dying words waved upon her aloft:

16 Now, behold, a thousand balls of iron skim the
surface of the waters, swift as shooting stars.

17 But when the battle waxed hot, and Perry saw
that the tackling of his vessel was shot away, and his men
were slain and wounded with great slaughter, and his destroying engines became silent,

18 He put the charge of the vessel into the hands of
one of his officers, whose name was Yarnell, a trusty man;

19 Then, with the starry banner of Columbia in his
hand, did the gallant Perry leap into his cock-boat, while
his brave mariners quickly conveyed him to another
fighting vessel of the United States called the Niagara,
commanded by a valiant man, whose name was Elliot.

20 After this again the vessels uttered their thunders
and fought hard, and the men of Columbia poured out
destruction upon the servants of the king.

21 And it came to pass, that the skilful contrivance of
Perry, and the bravery of his men, at length forced the
whole fleet of the king to become captive—even unto the
cock-boats of Columbia.

22 Thus again was the mighty lion humbled before
the eagle: for six strong vessels of Britain were overcome
at one time.

23 And the slain and wounded of the king that day, was about an hundred thirty and five; beside there were a thousand prisoners.

24 The loss of the United States was twenty and seven that were killed, and four score and ten were wounded.

25 Moreover, the number of the men of Britain made captive was more than all the men of Perry's squadron.

26 Now Perry was a righteous man, and like the good Samaritan, took care of the halt and maimed, and put skilful men to bind up their wounds; and the men of Britain blessed him.

27 Neither was he a man puffed up with vanity, even in the hour of victory;

28 For when he had conquered the fleet of Britain, he wrote to Jones,* one of the scribes of the great Sanhedrim, with modesty, saying,

29 To day it hath pleased the Lord that the people of Columbia should triumph over their enemies.

30 At the same time he wrote to Harrison, the chief captain of the host of Columbia, whose army was at the bay of Sandusky, saying, We have met the enemy, and they are ours!

31 Then did the enemies of Columbia weep; and the gainsayer put on deep mourning.

32 Moreover, the great Sanhedrim honored Perry with great honor; and gave him medals, with devices curiously wrought.

33 Likewise, the people gave him much silver plate, with gravings thereon, mentioning his deeds.

34 And the bye-stander might read his triumph in his country's eyes.

35 His sons shall hear him spoken of with pleasure, and his name shall be mentioned in the song of the virgins.

36 Where, oh! Bratain, are now thy mighty admirals? where thy Nelson? where the transcendant glory they gained for thee?

37 Alas! it hath expired upon the waters of Erie before the destroying engines of Perry!

---

* W. Jones, Secretary of the Navy.

CHAP. XXXII.

Capture of Malden and Detroit—the army of Gen. Proctor retreat towards the Moravian towns—Gen. Harrison pursues them.

NOW when Perry had taken care of the captives, and the wounded, and set them upon the shore,

2 He began to convey the army of Harrison from Fort Meigs and round about.

3 And having gathered them together into his vessels, he brought them, and landed them nigh unto the strong hold of Malden.

4 And it came to pass, on the twenty-third day of the same month, in which Perry conquered the fleet of Britain,

5 That Harrison, the chief captain, began to march the host of Columbia against the strong hold of Malden, and captured a town called Amherstburg, nigh thereunto.

6 Now Proctor was the chief captain of the savages and servants of the king.

7 And when he saw the men of Columbia approach, he destroyed the fort, the tents, and the store-houses of the king, and, with his whole host, fled swiftly towards Sandwich.

8 And Harrison, and the host of Columbia, followed hard after him.

9 Now when the savages of the wilderness beheld the men of Britain flee before the warriors of Columbia, their spirits sunk, and they were sore amazed.*

10 Moreover, they upbraided the servants of the king, saying, Lo! ye have deceived us, and led us from our hunting grounds, and we are an hungered.

11 For, verily, ye promised us bread and wine,† and silver and gold; yea, even that we should drink of the strong waters of Jamaica, if we would go out with you and fight the battles of the king, against the men of Columbia.

12 But, behold! now ye would run away and leave us to fight alone.

13 Whereupon many of their tribes cast away their tomahawks, and refused to fight under the banners of the king.

14 And when Harrison came to Sandwich, Proctor and his army had departed from the place. and fled towards the river Thames, near Moravian Town.

15 (Now the Thames emptieth its waters into the lake St. Clair. and the Moravian Towns lie upon the river, about an hundred miles from Malden, towards the north, in the province of Upper Canada.)

16 Moreover, as they journied on, the brave M'Arthur crossed over with his band to the strong hold of Detroit, and took it.

---

* *See Tecumseh's letter to Proctor.*

† *At this time the British army were short of supplies.*

17 But the savages and the men of Britain had destroyed those things which they could not carry away, and fled in haste.

18 So M'Arthur, in whom the chief captain put much faith, remained at Detroit in the charge thereof.

19 And it came to pass, when Harrison saw that the host of Britain fled before him, he departed from Sandwich and went after them ; it being on the second day of the next month.

20 And his whole army followed after him, in all about three thousand brave men from the back-woods of the state of Kentucky and the pleasant villages of Ohio.

21 Now Harrison was a mighty man of valor, and no man could make him afraid ; and the captains and officers that were with him were all valiant men.

22 And, when some of his captains said unto him, Lo ! there is a feast to day : go thou and partake thereof, and refresh thyself, and we will watch ;

23 He answered and said unto them, Nay, shall I go and riot, whilst the warriors of Columbia lie on the frozen ground ?

24 No, their fate shall be my fate ; and their glory shall be my glory.

25 So he wrapped himself in his cloak, and lay down in his own tent.

26 And the husbandmen of Kentucky were led on by their valiant governor, whose name was Shelby, and he was a man well stricken in years ; even at the age of threescore did he go out against the enemies of Columbia ; and all the people rejoiced in him.

27 And the gallant Perry staid not behind ; but freely offered his strength, and was one of the right hand men of Harrison, with whom he followed after the host of Britain.

28 Nevertheless, it happened that a band of the savages strove to give hindrance to the army of Columbia;

29 But the men of Columbia let two of the destroying engines loose upon them, and they fled into the wilderness like wild deer.

CHAP. XXXIII.

Battle of the Thames—Gen. Harrison captures the British army under Gen Proctor—illuminations on account of it—news of it received in England.

———

AND it came to pass, on the fifth day of the same month, that Proctor, with the savages and the army of the king, rested upon advantageous ground, on the banks of the river Thames,

2 Where he drew his army up in the order of battle, after the fashion of these days, and prepared himself to meet the host of Columbia.

3 Now the army of Proctor was mighty ; for he had a thousand horsemen : but the number of the savages that followed after him are not known to this time ; howbeit, they were many.

4 And they were under the charge of a chief warrior, whom they called Tecumseh, a savage whom the king had made a chief captain.*

5 And it came to pass, on the same day, in the latter part of the day, that the army of Harrison drew nigh unto the place.

———

** Brig. General.*

6 And he called together his captains of fifties, and his squadrons, and encouraged them, and commanded them to prepare themselves for the fight.

7 And he put the host of Columbia in battle array against the host of Britain, army against army.

8 Now the sound of the trumpet, the cymbal, the bugle-horn, and the noisy drum, echoed through the deep wilderness.

9 And the red savages appeared in the field before the men of Britain, for they had put them as a shield, in the front of the battle.

10 And they yelled with dreadful yellings, and sounded aloud the war-whoop, which was the signal of death.

11 But the army of Columbia rushed upon them with the fierceness of lions.

12 And the weapons of war were used without mercy; the foxes and the beavers crept into their holes, for the destroying engines frightened the wild beasts, so that they looked for their hiding places.

13 The gallant Johnson* fell upon them with a band of chosen horsemen, and he drove them before him like chaff before the wind, and smote their chief warrior,† and slew him with his own hand, so that he fell to the earth.

14 And the host of Columbia assailed the men of Britain on all sides, and overcame them, and made them prisoners of war; whereupon the engines ceased to utter their thunders.

---

* Col. Johnson, of the Kentucky light-horse.

† Tecumseh; who was at that moment in the act of shooting the colonel.

- 15 Howbeit, Proctor escaped, on a swift running horse, with a handful of his captains that were under him.

16 Now the number of prisoners captured by the army of Harrison that day were about six hundred.

17 And the slain and wounded of the men of Britain were thirty-and three; and the same number of savages were slain.

18 Of the army of Columbia seven were slain and two score and two were wounded.

19 But the men of Kentucky and Ohio, whose sons and brothers and fathers had been inhumanly slaughtered at the River Raisin, slew not a single captive.

20 But they treated them as MEN; thus rendering GOOD FOR EVIL, according to the word of the Lord.

21 Moreover, they captured six of the destroying engines that were made of brass, and two that were made of iron ; besides many weapons of war.

22 Now three of the brass engines were those given to the men of Britain, at the capture of Detroit, the first year of the war, and were the same that had been taken from the king in the days of WASHINGTON.

23 Soon after the battle, Harrison returned with his army to Detroit, where many of the savages had assembled, to repent of their evils, and ask for mercy from the chief captain.

24 So Harrison made a covenant with them, and they were thankful, and gave him hostages.

25 Now there were great rejoicings in the land of Columbia, and the hearts of the people were exceeding glad,

26 So that when the news thereof reached them they drank wine; and when the evening came they lighted their candles, and put them in candlesticks of silver and candlesticks of gold, and placed them in the windows of their houses.

27 And there were many thousands of them; and the light thereof was as though the stars had fallen from heaven.

28 This did they throughout the land of Columbia, from the district of Maine, in the east, to the state of Georgia, in the south.

29 And, when the Prince Regent, and the chief counsellors, and the wise men of Britain, heard the tidings, for a truth, that their fleet and their army were captured, they were astonished beyond measure.

30 They looked at one another like men who had lost their wits: they were silent, and their tongues clave to the roof of their mouths.

31 Their knees smote one against another, for the strength of Britain was shaken; her valiant warriors had lost their honour;* and her glory was outshone.

32 Now there was great honour and praise bestowed upon Harrison for his courage, and his valiant acts; and the people remembered his name with pleasure.

33 Moreover, he gave great praise to Shelby, the governor, and Perry, and Johnson, and all the brave men that were with him.

------

* *Doubly lost it: by water and by land; by being conquered, and by being cruel.*

34 And in the same month, when the object of the army was fulfilled, the husbandmen of Columbia returned every man to his own house.

35 But Harrison and Perry, and the band of warriors of the great Sanhedrim, went into their vessels.

36 And they moved from Detroit, and came in the ships of Perry, to Buffaloe, nigh unto the river Niagara, to meet Wilkinson, who came from the south, and was appointed chief captain of the army of the centre.

CHAP. XXXIV.

War with the Creek Nation of Indians—massacre at Fort Mimms—Georgia and Tennessee militia, under General Jackson retaliate.

NOW it came to pass, while these things were going on in the north, and the repentant savages laid their murderous weapons at the feet of Harrison,

2 That the servants of the king were stirring up the spirit of Satan in the savages of the wilderness of the south ;

3 And placing the destroying engines into their hands that they might shed the blood of the people of Columbia.

4 Now these southern barbarians were called the Creek nation of Indians.

5 Moreover, they were a nation of savages that dwelt in the back-woods and the wilderness round about the states of Georgia, Tennessee, and the Mississippi Territory.

6 So, about this time, they took their weapons of death in their hands, and went against the strong-hold of Fort Mimms, which lieth on a branch of the river

Mobile, that emptieth its waters into the great Gulf of Mexico.

7 And they captured the place ; and with the fury of demons they murdered, with the tomahawk, the men, the women, and the infants that were in and about the fort, sparing neither age nor sex ; and slaying the prisoners that begged for mercy.

8 And the number of the people of Columbia that were massacred and burnt alive in their houses, that day, was about four hundred ; however, there were an hundred savages slain.

9 For it was a sore fight ; and Beasly, who commanded the fort, fought hard against them ; howbeit, he was slain.

10 But it came to pass, in the same year, that the people of Columbia were revenged of the evil ;

11 Andrew, whose sir-name was Jackson, a man of courage and valor, was chief captain in the south ;

12 And he sent out one of his brave captains, whose name was Coffee, with a strong band ; even nine hundred mighty horsemen :

13 Now these were the valiant husbandmen of Georgia and the back-woods of Tennessee ; their horses were fleet as the roe-buck ; their weapons of war were certain death.

14 So they went forth against a town of the savages called Tallushatches, on the second day of the eleventh month.

15 And on the next day they encompassed the town round about ; and the savages prepared themselves for battle.

16 About the rising of the sun they sounded their drums, and began their horrible yellings.

17 But they frightened not the hearts of the brave men of Tennessee.

18 So when Coffee had stationed his captains and his men of war about the town, in the order of battle, the whole army shouted aloud ;

19 And the instruments of destruction were let loose upon them on all sides ; and they fought with all their might.

20 But the men of Columbia rushed upon them, and subdued them, and made about four score women and children captive.

21 And slew about two hundred of their warriors ; leaving not a man to tell the tidings.

22 For, lo ! when the savages of the wilderness commit great evils and transgressions against the people of Columbia,

23 The great Sanhedrim of the people send out mighty armies against them, that are able to overthrow them, and make their towns a desolation, and lay waste their habitations.

24 Now the loss of the army of Columbia that day, was five slain and about forty wounded.

25 And Jackson, the chief captain, gave great praise to Coffee, and all the valiant men that fought that day.

26 On the next day after the battle, the army of Columbia returned to their camp, at a place called the Ten-Islands.

CHAP. XXXV.

Continuation of the War with the Creeks—Gen. Jackson's great victory over them—they suc for peace—a treaty is concluded with them.

————

NOTWITHSTANDING their discomfiture, the nation of the Creeks were still bent on warring against the people of Columbia.

2 And they committed many outrages upon the inhabitants of the states round about.

3 But it came to pass, on the seventh day of the same month, that a messenger came to Jackson, the chief captain, and spake unto him, saying :

4 Lo ! even now, more than a thousand savages have pitched their tents at Talledoga, near the strong hold of Lashley, with intent to assail it.

5 Immediately Jackson took two thousand hardy men, who were called volunteers, because they had, unsolicited, offered their services to their country, and led them against the savages.

6 Now, the men of war that followed after him were mostly from the state of Tennessee, and men of dauntless courage.

7 So, early in the morning of the next day, the army of Jackson drew nigh the place, in battle array.

8 And the savages came out towards the army of Columbia, with shouting and yellings : and again the engines of destruction were used plentifully.

9 And the leaden balls whizzed about their ears like unto a nest of hornets.

10 But the horsemen, and the whole army of Jackson, rushed upon the savages, and slew them with great slaughter, and overcame them.

11 And the number of savages slain that day was about three hundred; and a red-cross banner of the Spanish nation was found amongst them, and taken.

12 Seventeen of the men of Columbia were slain and about four score wounded.

13 So, when the battle was over, Jackson returned to his own camp.

14 After these things had come to pass, on the twelfth day of the month, a certain captain, whose sir-name was White, was sent against another place called the Hillabee-Towns.

15 And, on the eighteenth day of the same month, he took the towns, and destroyed them, and slew three score of the savages, and made about two hundred two score and ten prisoners.

16 About eleven days afterwards, a valiant captain, whose name was Floyd, with his brave men, went against the towns of Autossee and Tallisee, which lie on the banks of the river Tallapoosie.

17 And Floyd went against them with boldness and triumphed over them and killed about two hundred of them, and burned their towns with fire, and slew the king of Autossee, and the king of Tallisee, who were the kings of two tribes.

18 Moreover, on the thirteenth day of the next month, Claiborne, a governor, and a man of valor, went against the savages that dwelt on the river Alabama.

19 And he marched with his army through the wilderness more than an hundred miles, to a town built upon a place called by the savages the Holy-Ground, where three of the Indian prophets dwelt.

20 Now there were lying prophets among the savages, even as there were in the days of old, among the children of Israel; and they prophesied according to their own wishes;

21 And those of shallow understanding believed them, and were led into a snare, whereby their whole tribe was nigh being destroyed.

22 And Wetherford, the chief warrior of the Creek nation, was there also with his band.

23 And he fought hard against Claiborne; but he was overthrown, and fled, and the town was burnt, even two hundred houses.

24 Notwithstanding all these tribulations, the depredations of the savages of the south were not stayed.

25 So Jackson, the chief captain, went out against them with his army, and attacked them at their strong hold, on the waters of the Tallapoosie, where they were entrenched, with more than a thousand warriors.

26 Now this was on the twenty and seventh day of the third month, in the one thousand eight hundred and fourteenth year of the christian era.

27 And Jackson set his destroying engines to work, and fought desperately against them, for about the space

MAJ.^R GEN.^L ANDREW JACKSON

(of the United States Army).

Engraved for Hunt's history of the War.

of five hours; when he overcame them, so that only
about a score escaped.

28 Seven hundred and fifty of the savage warriors
were found slain in battle; and two hundred two score
and ten women and children became captives to the
army of Columbia.

29 Manahoee, their chief prophet, was smitten in
the mouth, and slain, and two other false prophets
were slain with him.

30 Moreover, about the first day of the sixth month,
a brave man, whose name was Pearson, with the husbandmen of the states, of North and South Carolina,
went against them along the borders of the Alabama, and
captured about six hundred of them.

31 Thus did the men of Columbia triumph over
them, and conquer them, even to the seventh time.

32 And so the judgment of the Lord fell upon them
for their unrighteousness, and for their wicked and murderous deeds.

33 After which they repented of their evil, having,
through their own folly, lost many thousand warriors.

34 And their chief warriors gave up their instruments of destruction, and laid them at the feet of
Jackson, the chief captain.

35 Even Wetherford, the chief warrior, gave himself up to Jackson, saying, I fought with my might; but
I have brought evil upon my nation; and thou hast
slain my warriors; and I myself am overcome

36 Now the savages are easily inflamed and roused to
works of sin and death; and of their weakness the servants of the king are not ashamed to take advan-

tage; even to the ruin of the poor and ignorant barbarians.

37 So the warriors and the whole nation of the Creeks, being tired of a destructive war, entreated the men of Columbia for peace, saying unto Jackson,

38 Lo! now are our eyes opened to our own profit; now will we make peace with you.

39 And if ye will no more suffer the fire, and the sword, and the destroying engines to spread desolation amongst us,

40 Then will we make a covenant with you, and give you for an inheritance a great part of the land which our fathers inherited before us.

41 And the length and the breadth thereof shall be about as large as the whole island of Britain, whose men of war have led us into this snare.

42 For although the king, who calleth himself our father, across the great waters, did put the instruments of death into our hands, and give us the black dust in abundance; nevertheless, he deceived us; and in the hour of danger his servants left us to take care of ourselves.

43 So Jackson made a covenant with them; and it was signed by the chiefs of their nation. _

44 And after it had been examined by the wise men and the great Sanhedrim of the people, it was ratified and signed with the hand-writing of James, the chief governer of the land of Columbia.

CHAP. XXXVI.

Plan of attack on Montreal defeated.

THE frailty of man speaketh volumes ; one man ac-
cuseth another ; but where is he who is perfect?

2 Man deviseth mighty plans in his own mind, but
he accomplisheth them not.

3 He is wise in his own conceit, but his wisdom
faileth him : he seeth folly in others, but perceiveth not
his own ; he is as a reed shaken with the wind.

4 Now the country of Columbia was assailed on every
side by the enemies of freedom.

5 And in the hope that the war might speedily cease,
and an end be made of the shedding of blood, the great
Sanhedrim of the people wished to push their armies
into the heart of the provinces of the king, even to
Montreal.

6 So they pitched upon certain chief captains, who
were well skilled in the arts of warfare : and Wilkinson
and Hampton were the names of the captains ;

7 And Brown, and Boyd, and Covington, and Swift,
and Coles, and Purdy, and Ripley, and Swartwout,
and Fraser, and many others, were valiant captains under them.

8 Not many days after Harrison returned from his
triumph over Proctor's army ; and in the same year,

it came to pass, that Wilkinson conveyed his army from Fort George and the country of Niagara, to Sackett's Harbor, at the east end of lake Ontario; leaving Harrison and M'Clure behind, at the strong hold of Fort George.

9 From Sackett's Harbor Wilkinson moved to a place called Grenadier Island; and in the first week of the eleventh month he arrived at Ogdensburgh, in order to go against the strong hold of Montreal.

10 Now the army of Hampton rested nigh unto lake Champlain; and about the same time he moved towards the borders of the king.

11 And Wilkinson sent a messenger to him, and entreated him to come and meet him, and join the two armies at the village of St. Regis.

12 The same night Wilkinson with his army crossed the great river St. Lawrence, near by the strong hold of Prescot, which lieth in the dominions of the king.

13 And he moved down with about six thousand men towards the hold of Montreal, until he came to a place called Crystler's Farms, nigh unto Williamsburgh.

14 Now, at this place, on the eleventh day of the eleventh month, a strong band of the men of war of Britain, from Kingston and round about, fell upon his army in the rear, and annoyed them greatly.

15 At length, on the same day, a part of the army of Columbia turned about, and fought against them and drove them back; however it was a sore fight.

16 Wilkinson, the chief captain, who went before the host of Columbia, had been sick many days, and was unable to go forth against them himself.

17 So he sent some of his brave captains, even Boyd, and Swartwout, and Covington; and the engines of destruction were set to work with great noise and fury; and the valiant Covington was wounded unto death.

18 Moreover, the loss of the men of Columbia that day was an hundred slain, and two hundred two score and ten wounded, and the loss of the king was about an hundred four score and one.

19 After this battle the army of Wilkinson moved along the St. Lawrence until they came to Barnheart's, near Cornwall, where they met the valiant Brown.

20 Now this place lieth on the north side of the river, and on the other side lieth St. Regis, where Wilkinson, the chief captain, expected to be joined by the army of Hampton, from Champlain.

21 But in this he was disappointed; for, lo! Hampton sent one of his captains, whose name was Atkinson, to Wilkinson, with the tidings that he had declined to meet him, and was returning to his camp on the lake.

22 Now when the army of Wilkinson heard those things, they were discouraged; and all the plans that had been devised by Armstrong,* the chief captain, and scribe of the great Sanhedrim, were of no avail.

23 So the army of Wilkinson crossed the river again and came into the land of Columbia, at French Mills, near St. Regis; where they went into winter quarters.

---

* *Gen. Armstrong, Secretary at War.*

24 And the men of Columbia, even the great Sanhedrim, were disappointed in their expectations.

25 Moreover, Hampton received much blame in the
thing ; and he was even taxed with the crime of drink
ing too freely of the strong waters.

26 But the imaginary evils which the children of men
commit are oftentimes graven in brass, whilst their actual
good deeds are written in sand.

27 Neither shall it be forgotten here, that, when the
shivering soldiers of Columbia were suffering with cold
in the north,

28 The lovely and patriotic daughters of Columbia,
blest with tenderness, remembered them, and sent them
coverings for their hands and their feet :

29 Even from the fleece of their fathers' flocks, they
wrought them with their own hands, and distributed
them with a good heart.

30 And, for their kindness and humanity, the poor
soldier blessed them, and their virtues were extolled by
the men of Columbia throughout the land.

CHAP. XXXVII.

Newark burnt—Fort George evacuated—Niagara frontier laid waste—Buffaloe burnt.

———

IN the meantime, however, the strong vessels of Chauncey went out and brought Harrison, and the remnant of his army, from Fort George to Sackett's Harbor, to protect the place.

2 But they left M'Clure behind, with the men under him; being for the most part husbandmen, called militia, and volunteers.

3 And they were eager to be led on to the battle; but the term for which their services were engaged having expired, they returned every man to his own house.

4 So M'Clure, the chief captain of the fort, called a council of his officers, and they agreed to depart to the strong hold of Niagara.

5 And they took their destroying engines and the black dust, and the bread and meat of the army, and carried them across the river.

6 Likewise they put a lighted match to the black dust in the fort, and it was rent asunder with a great noise, as it were of thunder and an earthquake.

7 Moreover, they burnt the town of Newark, before they departed, which happened on the tenth day of the twelfth month.

8 Howbeit, they gave the inhabitants time to save themselves, before they put the burning torch to their dwellings; nevertheless, it was an evil thing, and pleased not the people of Columbia.

9 The men of Columbia were not cruel, and they put none of the inhabitants of the town to the sword.

10 After this, it came to pass, on the nineteenth day of the same month, early in the morning. before the dawning of the day, about fifteen hundred of the savages and soldiers of the king crossed the river, and went against Niagara.

11 And they fell unawares upon the men of Columbia, while they were yet asleep in their tents; and overcame them, and took the fort, and put the garrison to the sword; even the women and children suffered under the savage tomahawk.

12 Now the people of Columbia, who were massacred that day, were about two hundred two score and ten.

13 But the captain of the hold, whose name was Leonard, was charged with the evil; for he had left the fort, and neglected that duty which should ever be the pride of a soldier.

14 Nevertheless, when they had committed all this horrid slaughter, the barbarians were not fully glutted with murder;

15 So they went against the little villages of Lewistown, Manchester, Youngstown, and Tuscarora, and burnt them with fire, and slew the poor and helpless that dwelt round about the place.

16 After which, at the close of the year, they went against the beautiful village of Buffaloe, and burnt it also; and made it a ruin and a desolation.

CHAP. XXXVIII.

Cruise of the U. S. frigate Essex, D. Porter commander—her defence and capture, at Valparaiso.

NOW whilst the great lakes and rivers were bound in fetters of ice, and the arms of Columbia slumbered in the winter camps of the north;

2 And whilst the conquering sword of Jackson spread ruin and desolation among the misguided savages of the south;

3 Lo! new scenes of warfare appeared upon the waters of the great deep.

4 In the first year of the war David, whose sirname was Porter, sailed from the shores of Columbia towards the south, that he might capture the vessels of the men of Britain.

5 And the ship which he commanded was one of the strong vessels of Columbia, called the Essex.

6 Now David was a valiant man, and he had contrived a plan to annoy the commerce of Britain in the waters of the great Pacific Ocean.

7 So, in process of time, he passed around the furthermost part of the land of Columbia, which is called Cape Horn, and lieth far to the south; near the country of Patagonia, which is inhabited by the barbarians, and sailed towards the haven of Valparaiso.

From whence, leaving Chili to the south, he moved along the coast of Peru, till he came to Lima, where it never rains :

9 A country where gold and silver are found in abundance, and where there is one continual summer, and the trees blossom throughout the year.

10 Again, he prepared his vessels, and sailed from Lima towards the north, until he fell upon the islands of Gallapagos ; called the enchanted islands.

11 Now these islands lie upon the west side of the great continent of Columbia, under a meridian sun, beneath the girdle of the world.

12 Hereabouts he captured a multitude of the merchant ships of Britain, laden with rich merchandize, and silver and gold.

13 And he fixed a score of the destroying engines into one of the ships he had taken; and made her a fighting vessel, and called her name Essex Junior, and a man, whose name was Downs, he made captain thereof.

14 And he fell upon the fishermen of Britain, and captured those who went out to catch the mighty whales, which afford oil to give us light in the night time, and bones to shade our daughters from the scorching sun of the noon-day.

15 Moreover, David went to an island where dwelt wild savages, and established himself, so that he could go out and return, whensoever he chose.

16 And when he departed from the island, which he called after the chief governor of the land of Columbia

in those days,* he left some of his men, with the weapons of war to defend the place.

17 Now David was a grievous thorn in the side of Britain, and he almost destroyed her whole commerce in the South Seas :

18 Inasmuch as he put the wise men of the king to their wits end; for they were unable to out-sail him and take him captive.

19 So they sent their strong ships in search of him, by two's, over the whole face of the waters of the Southern Ocean; and the expense thereof would have made more than two feasts for the Prince Regent, who governed England in the name of his father.

20 However, it came to pass, that David returned again in his ship to the haven of Valparaiso; and the vessel, called the Essex Junior, accompanied him.

21 Now Downs, who commanded her, had been to the place before, and conducted the prizes of David there, and brought him the tidings that he was likely to be en-snared upon the waters.

22 So, whilst David was there, on the twenty-eighth day of the third month, in the eighteen hundred and fourteenth year of the Christian era,

23 He looked around, and behold! he saw two of the strong ships of Britain approaching, for the purpose of hemming him in; the one called the Phœbe, and the other the Cherub.

24 But his heart sank not within him, for he knew no cowardice; but, with the wisdom of a brave man,

----

* *Madison Island.*

he strove to escape, as the vessels were too powerful for him.

25 But the winds were adverse, and blew hard, and prevented the tacklings of his ship from taking effect :

26 Nevertheless, David said unto the captains of the king, Come singly, and not like cowards, upon me ; then shall ye receive the thunders of the freemen of Columbia abundantly ;

27 And her fame shall not suffer, although in the contest ye may destroy my vessel upon the face of the waters.

28 But Hillyar, the captain of the king's ship called the Phœbe, was afraid lest he should be overcome.

29 Now, when David found he was unable to make good his escape, he drew nigh the land, that he might be protected by the great law of nations; for it was a place friendly to both parties.

30 But in this he was deceived; for the authorities of Spain trembled at the nod of the servants of Britain, in whom there was no faith.

31 So both vessels came upon him, like ravenous wolves, in the very haven of Valparaiso ; thus transgressing the law of nations, and committing an outrage which hath few examples under the sun.

32 And they set their engines to work upon the Essex with all their might.

33 Nevertheless, David fought against them with desperation, for there was no hope left for him to escape ; neither did he expect mercy.

34 And he held out for more than the space of two hours, when he became overpowered ; having his ship a sinking wreck, covered with blood, and on fire ; with

about an hundred and fifty of his men slain and maim
ed :

35 So, after David had fought hard, he became captive to the ships of the king; who had also some of
their men slain, and some wounded.

36 Moreover, Hillyar gave him praise and called
him a man of courage; for he fought against two strong
ships of Britain.

37 And David made a covenant with Hillyar, in
which the Essex Junior was given unto him and his
men, that they might return in her again to their own
country.

38 And it came to pass, in the seventh month of
the same year of the battle, David arrived in the city
of New-York; having been absent about two years.

39 Now when the people of Columbia beheld the
valiant Porter, they were rejoiced with exceeding great
oy; inasmuch as they unharnessed the horses from before his chariot, and drew him through the city.

40 And they made a sumptuous feast for him, and
invited a multitude of guests; and spent the day in gladness and mirth.

CHAP. XXXIX.

Capture of the U. S. sloop of war Frolic, by the British frigate Orpheus—capture of the British sloop of war L'Epervier, by the Peacock, Capt. Warrington—capture of the Reindeer, by the Wasp, Capt. Blakely—the Avon captured and sunk—U. S. vessels Syren and Rattlesnake captured—Admiral Cochrane declares the whole American coast in a state of blockade.

———

NOW it happened on the twenty-first day of the fourth month of the eighteen hundred and fourteenth year, that one of the strong ships of the king, called the Orpheus;

2 Being upon the waters of the great deep, fell in with a small vessel of the United States, called the Frolic, and made capture thereof.

3 However, in the same month, not many days afterwards, a fighting vessel of Columbia, called the Peacock, commanded by the brave Warrington, met one of the vessels of the king.

4 Now they were about equal in force; and the name of the vessel of Britain was called L'Epervier and the captain's name was Wales.

5 And they sat the engines of destruction to work, and fought with great fury for the space of forty minutes;

6 When the mariners of Columbia overcame the servants of the king, and the vessel of Britain struck her red-cross to the ship of Warrington.

7 And there were slain and wounded of the servants of the king about twenty and three; but there were none slain of the people of Columbia.

8 Moreover, Warrington gat about an hundred and twenty thousand pieces of silver, that were in the vessel.

9 And he received great praise throughout the land for this gallant exploit.

10 And the great Sanhedrin thanked him and gave him a medal of gold.

11 Likewise, the people of Savannah, a chief town in the state of Georgia, being a thousand miles to the south of New-York, honored him greatly.

12 For he had brought both vessels into their port; and there were much rejoicings; and a rich feast was prepared for him by the people.

13 Moreover, it came to pass, on the twenty-eighth day of the sixth month, that one of the fighting ships of Columbia, called the Wasp, met a vessel of the king, upon the ocean, called the Reindeer; after one of the swift running animals of Columbia.

14 Now the Wasp was commanded by a man of courage, whose name was Blakely.

15 And a dreadful battle began; and the mischievous balls of destruction showered around with tremendous noise.

16 Nevertheless, Blakely ran down upon the Reindeer, and in about twenty minutes he captured her.

17 But her captain was slain; and she was as it

were a wreck upon the waters; so Blakely destroyed her.

18 The loss of the king, in killed and wounded that day, was about seventy and five; and five of the men of Columbia were slain, and about a score maimed.

19 And the friends of the great Sanhedrim were pleased with the valiant acts of Blakely.

20 Moreover, on the twenty-seventh day of the eighth month, the Wasp captured another ship of the king, called the Avon, and sunk her to the bottom of the great deep.

21 And the slain and wounded of the Avon, was two score and two.

22 Howbeit, about the same time, the Syren and the Rattlesnake* fell into the hands of the king.

23 About this time, the whole land of Columbia was ordered to be hemmed in by Cochrane, a servant of the king, and a chief captain of the navy of Britain.

24 But all their blockades were of no avail; for the men of Columbia escaped and outwitted them.

** U. S. schooner and brig, about 14 guns each.*

CHAP. XL.

*Breaking up of the cantonment at French Mills—
affair at La-Cole-Mill—Major Appling captures
two hundred British seamen—Gen. Brown captures
Fort Erie—battle of Chippawa plains.*

———

NOW it came to pass, in the second month of the
same year in which David gat home to the United
States,

2 That the armies of the north began to be in motion,
and departed from the place called French Mills,
where they were encamped.

3 And a part thereof moved towards Plattsburgh, on
lake Champlain; and was commanded by a brave man,
whose name was Macomb, and Wilkinson, the chief
captain, followed after them.

4 But the other part of the host, commanded by
Jacob, whose sir-name was Brown, went to Sackett's
Harbor; and from thence against the strong hold of
Niagara.

5 And it was so, that when Wilkinson heard that
Jacob had gone against Niagara; he marshalled out
his force, and went against a place in the province of
the king, called La-Cole-Mill, to take it.

6 Nevertheless, he failed, and lost many men; after
which the command of the army was given to a chief
captain, whose name was Izard.

7 In the meanwhile many of the evils of warfare were committed on and about the waters of Ontario and the great lake Erie.

8 And a gallant captain, whose name was Appling,* took about two hundred of the mariners of the royal navy of Britain, at a place called Sandy-Creek, by the waters of lake Ontario: being in the same month that the strong hold of Oswego was taken by the men of Britain.

9 Now on the third day of the seventh month, it came to pass, that Jacob, the chief captain of the host of Columbia, on the borders of the river Niagara,

10 Having prepared his men beforehand, crossed the river and captured fort Erie, and an hundred thirty and seven of the soldiers of the king, and some of the destroying engines ;

11 And the next day being the anniversary of the independence of Columbia, after having left some of the men of war to defend the place,

12 He moved with his host towards the plains of Chippawa, where they rested for the night.

13 On the next day Jacob assembled his captains of fifties, and his captains of hundreds, and spake unto them, saying,

14 Lo! the army of the king are mighty men of valor, and their numbers are great, even those who fought in Spain, under the banners of Welling-

---

* *Major Appling.*

ton,* the chief warrior of Britain; and Riall, the chief captain of the host, is a man of great experience:

15 Nevertheless, be not disheartened; but let us beware that we be not ensnared.

16 So he prepared his army to go against the host of Britain, in battle array; and the soldiers of Columbia shouted for the battle.

17 Now the army of Britain rested upon the plains of Chippawa, and were ready to meet the army of Columbia; they shouted aloud, and inflamed their blood with the strong waters of Jamaica.

18 And they put fire to the black dust of the destroying engines; and a great noise issued from the mouths thereof.

19 Moreover, they vomited fire and smoke and brimstone incessantly, and with the movements of the armies the dust of the earth arose and overshadowed the field of slaughter.

20 And the heavy balls of iron whistled about them in abundance.

21 However, the skill of Jacob, and his brave captains, became manifest, and they drove the host of Britain before them,

22 And compelled them to flee to their strong entrenchments at Fort George and Fort Niagara.

23 And the field of battle was covered with the slain and the maimed; even eight hundred men.

24 And the slain and wounded of the servants of the king were about five hundred.

* *Lord Wellington.*

25 So Jacob and his army gat great praise, and a
the warriors of Columbia that fought that day :

26 Amongst whom were the volunteers of the
states of New-York and Pennsylvania, who were led
on by the gallant Porter.*

27 And Ripley was there, and the brave Scott, who
went out and fought in the heat of the battle.

** Gens. Porter, Ripley, and Scott*

CHAP. XLI.

Battle of Bridgewater.

NOW about this time there was peace among the strong powers of Europe; and the strength of Britain was free to be employed against the people of Columbia.

2 So she increased her navy on the shores of Columbia, and strengthened her armies in Canada; and sent skilful men to conduct them and to fight her battles :

3 And, in her spite, she emptied out the vials of her vengeance upon the United States.

4 Notwithstanding, it came to pass, on the twenty fifth day of the same month,

5 That another bloody battle was fought hard by, at a place called Bridgewater, from whence ye might behold the stupendous water-falls of Niagara.

6 There the army of Britain came out against Jacob, with a host of five thousand chosen men.

7 Now the numbers of the host of Columbia were less than the host of the king, who were commanded by two chief captains, the one named Drummond,* and the other Riall;

---

* *Gen. Drummond.*

8 Nevertheless, Jacob went out against them and gave them battle : and the army of· Columbia shouted aloud; and the battle waxed hot beyond measure.

9 And it lasted for the space of seven hours ; even until the midnight.

10 The huge engines of destruction roared as the loud thunder, and the blaze thereof was like unto flashes of lightning.

11 But it came to·pass, that the army of Columbia drove the invincibles of Wellington from the field.

12 The valiant Miller, with his band, rushed upon the soldiers of the king, with the sharp points of his weapons of war, that faintly glittered in the light of the moon, and overcame them.*

13 Moreover, Drummond, the·chief captain of the king, was wounded, and in danger of being made captive; and Riall, the chief captain, was taken and fell into the hands of the brave Jessup.†

14 And Jacob, the chief captain of the host of Columbia, was sorely wounded; and the brave Scott was wounded also.

15 However, this was a dreadful battle, fought army against army, and blood and slaughter covered the green fields.

16 The loss of the king, was about a thousand and two hundred fighting men, who came to lose in the land of Columbia the honor they won in Europe.

---

* *Miller's brilliant charge on the enemy.*

† *Major Jessup, of the 25th Reg.*

17 The loss of the men of Columbia was also very great; being an hundred three score and ten slain, and more than five hundred maimed.

18 Now, as Jacob, the chief captain of the host of Columbia, was wounded, the charge was given to the valiant Ripley, and the army returned to the strong hold of Fort Erie.

19 And Jacob and his brave men gained great praise throughout the land of Columbia.

CHAP. XLII.

Assault on Fort Erie, by the British, under Gen. Drummond—Gen. Brown resumes his command—sallies out of Fort Erie against the British camp—M'Arthur's expedition into Canada.

AND it came to pass, on the fourth day of the next month, being the same day that the gallant Morgan, with two hundred and two score men, drove a thousand soldiers of the king from before Black Rock,

2 That a chief captain of Columbia whose name was Gaines,* arrived from Sackett's, Harbor at Fort Erie; and took the command thereof.

3 And it was so, that on the following day the army of the king approached towards the fort, and encamped themselves.

4 Moreover, they threw up breast-works and prepared their battering-rams, with intent to destroy the place, and make captives of the men of Columbia.

5 And on the fifteenth day of the month, after they had prepared themselves, they rushed forth with all their might against the strong hold of Columbia.

6 And as their deeds were evil, they began in the dead of the night, when the howlings of the wild wolf

* Gen. Gaines.
O

are heard from afar, and the steady roar of distant wa-ter-falls, catches the ear of the drowsy centinel.

7 Lo! it was a night dark and gloomy; and the very clouds of heaven wept for the folly of man.*

8 Quickly did the weapons of murder disturb and trouble the general silence.

9 Their thunders roared around the battlements; and the sudden blaze, from the engines, was as a thousand flashes of lightning.

10 But the men of Columbia were not asleep; for they met them at the onset: thrice the men of Britain came; and thrice were they driven back.

11 About this time, a man of Columbia, who was sorely wounded, begged of an officer of the king that his life might be spared;

12 But the captain, whose name was Drummond,† to whom he spake, refused him quarters; and, taking an oath, he swore, and cursed the men of Columbia, saying, Even as I slay thee, so shall it be with ye all.

13 Thus violating the commandment of God, which sayeth, Thou shalt do no murder.

14 But the hand of the Lord was stretched out against him; for while he was yet speaking, in the wickedness of his heart, he was smitten dead to the earth.

15 Now, although the men of Britain did some injury to the fort, they were quickly compelled to depart.

----

* *It was a rainy night.*

† *Col. Drummond.*

16 And the slain and wounded of the king that night, were about seven hundred, besides two hundred captives.

17 The loss of the United States was about an hundred men.

18 Now it came to pass, on the seventeenth day of the next month, when Jacob was recovered of his wounds, and had resumed his command, he sallied out of Fort Erie with his men, and went against the camp of the servants of the king.

19 And by his bravery and skill, and that of the valiant captains under him, he took and destroyed their strong holds, and slew many of them, so that their loss was about a thousand fighting men.

20 And the slain and wounded of Jacob's army were two hundred ninety and nine.

21 Now the valiant deeds of Jacob, and his brave men, are they not written in all the books of the chronicles of the land of Columbia of that day ?

22 After this, on the twenty-first day of the same month, the chief captain, and the host of Britain, being tired of the noise of the destroying engines of the men of Columbia, went away from the place and rested at Queenstown.

23 About this time Izard, the chief captain, arrived at Fort Erie, from Plattsburgh, and, as he was the oldest captain, he took the charge of the army of the north.

24 During these circumstances, it happened that the brave M'Arthur, who had remained at the strong hold of Detroit, to defend it,

25 Moved his army towards Burlington Heights.
and went more than an hundred miles into the province
of Canada.

26 And the men of Columbia that went with him
were valiant men, from the states of Kentucky and Ohio ;
in number about eight hundred.

27 Victory perched upon their arms, and they slew
some of the servants of the king, and made many
prisoners, and returned again with the loss of one man.

28 In the meanwhile, the army of Izard crossed the
river and returned from Erie to the borders of Columbia,
in the latter part of the year, and went into their winter
camps at Buffalo.

CHAP. XLIII.

Attack on Stonington, by the British ships of war which are defeated and driven off.

———

IN these days the strong powers of Britain strove hard to quench the fire of Columbian Liberty,

2 But it was lighted up by the hand of heaven, and not to be extinguished.

3 Now it came to pass, on the ninth day of the eighth month of the same year,

4 That the mighty ships of Britain came and opened their thundering engines upon the little town of Stonington, which lieth in the state of Connecticut, in the east.

5 But the inhabitants of the place were bold and valiant men, and they scorned to make a covenant with the servants of the king.

6 Although Hardy,* the chief captain of the king's ships had threatened to destroy the place; saying, Remove from the town your women and your children, who are innocent and fight not.

7 Thus shewing more righteousness than any of the

———

* *Com Hardy, a captain under Lord Nelson, at the battle of Trafalgar.*

king's captains: albeit, he gave them only the space of one hour to depart: ,

8 So the men of Columbia let the destroying engines loose upon the vessels, and shot the yankee balls amongst them plentifully, and compelled them to depart:

9 Notwithstanding, they had but two of the destroying engines in the place.

10 However, on the eleventh day of the same month, they were again forced to put them in motion.

11 For, in the meantime, Hardy had sent a messenger to the inhabitants, saying,

12 If ye will not prove wicked, and will refrain from sending your evil torpedoes amongst our vessels, then will we spare your town.

13 Now Hardy was mightily afraid of these torpedoes, (the history whereof is written in the fiftieth book of these chronicles) and he trembled at the sound of the name thereof.

14 Nevertheless, the people of Stonington refused his request.

15 So the ships of Britain came again and they brought another strong ship of the king to help them to take the place.

16 But once more the valiant sons of Connecticut made them fly for safety: and they came not again.

17 And the gallant conduct of the people of Stonington gained them much praise, even from the great Sanhedrim of the people.

18 Thus would the men of Columbia have done, in many other places, but for the false words and wickedness of traitorous men.

CHAP. XLIV.

Affairs in the Chesapeake—British army move up the Patuxent—land and march towards the city of Washington—prepare themselves for battle at Bladensburgh.

———

NOW the mighty fleet of Britain, that troubled the waters of the great Bay of Chesapeake, commanded by Cockburn the wicked, continued their depredations.

2 The number of their fighting ships were increased, and the soldiers of the king had come thither in multitudes from the island of Britain.

3 For the war which she had waged against the mighty ruler of France,* was at an end; and all their men of war were idle; so they sent them against the men of Columbia, who slew them with terrible slaughter.

4 Now the numbers of the servants and soldiers of the king, in and about the Chesapeake, were little fewer than ten thousand.

5 And they moved up the great river, which is called the Potowmac, and the river Patuxent, which lieth to the east thereof.

6 So, as they passed along, they did much damage;

———

* *Buonaparte.*

CHAP. XLV.

*Capture of Washington—Sacking of Alexandria—
death of Sir Peter Parker.*

Now, when Ross, the chief captain, had done speaking, they sent forth their fire brands, and sat their destroying engines to work, and cast balls of destruction and death.

2 Nevertheless, the men of Columbia were not dismayed, but poured out their thunders upon them in abundance.

3 And Joshua, sir-named Barney, who commanded the vessels of Columbia near the place, with his brave men, went out upon the land, and fought against them with desperation.

4 For he had ordered his little fleet to be burnt with fire, that the men of Britain might not profit thereby, and it blew up in the air with a loud noise.

5 Now Joshua was in the heat of the battle; and his destroying engines slew the men of Britain on all sides: however, he was wounded and made captive.

6 But the servants of the king treated Joshua well, and honoured him for his bravery.

7 Now James, the chief governor, and the counsellors, and the scribes of the great Sanhedrim, went out

to see the battle, and to contrive for the safety of the city.

8 And Munroe,* the chief scribe of the great Sanhedrim, was there; and Armstrong,† and many other friends of the land of Columbia.

9 Nevertheless, the wisdom of all their plans failed them; and they were sorely grieved to behold the husbandmen and the army of Winder, the chief captain, flee before the host of Britain.

10 But they were misled in their calculations; and they were now unable to prevent the evil.

11 Neither did the men of war they counted upon arrive in time to catch the army of the king.

12 Therefore, the host of Columbia fled, and went beyond the city, and passing through Georgetown, rested at a place called Montgomery Court-house.

13 And the slain and maimed of the king, were about four hundred: those of the men of Columbia about two score.

14 Now it was about the going down of the sun, when the host of the king polluted the Citadel of Freedom, and with their unhallowed footsteps violated the Temple of Liberty.

15 And Cockburn and Ross led the savage band of Britain into the midst of the city.

16 And the men of Columbia gnashed their teeth, as

the

* Hon. James Munroe, then Sec'ry of State.
† Gen. Armstrong.

bit their lips with vexation; for the thing might have been prevented.*

17 Nevertheless, it proved a blessing; for it united the people of Columbia as one man, against the tyrants of the earth.

18 Now the place that had been pitched upon to build the chief city, was in a fine country, and a beautiful spot, in the District of Columbia.

19 But the inhabitants round about the City of Washington were few; for they had, as it were, just began to build it.

20 There was much ground laid out for the city, but the buildings therein were not many; neither was it fortified.

Whatever may be individual sentiment, it has been, and still is the opinion of the best informed, that there was sufficient time to have had the place entrenched and fortified, if necessary, with an hundred pieces of cannon; and at least to have kept the enemy at bay, until a sufficient force were assembled to have cut off his retreat. But to expect raw militia to meet and repulse, in an open plain, solid columns of regular troops, superior in numbers as well as discipline, must be preposterous. Who is to blame in the business we presume not to say; but hope a recurrence of the evil may be provided against in future. Had the same energy and industry been exercised at the city of Washington, that were displayed by the patriotic citizens of New-York, in erecting fortifications for the defence of their capital, we might have been spared the mortification that followed the capture of the seat of government.

21 So when the servants of the king came to the place, they looked around, in surprise, and cried out with astonishment, saying,

22 Lo! the city hath fled with the people, for there are but an handful of houses in the place.

23 However, the next day they began the work of destruction, like unto the barbarians of ancient times; for their wickedness followed after them as the shadow followeth after the substance.

24 And they destroyed the beautiful edifices with fire, even the palace of the great Sanhedrim.

25 Now Cockburn was loath that his wicked deeds should be handed down to future generations; so he went and destroyed, with his own hands, the chief printing-office* of the city, and scattered the types abroad;

26 Because, as he alledged, the printer had, in times past, uttered many hard things against him.

27 Thus did he, even Cockburn, like an ignorant savage, stamp his own name with infamy, and make it become a reproach amongst all mankind.

28 Science and learning blushed at the champions of England, who had been represented as the bulwark of religion; but who were, in reality, the supporters of idolatry; the staff of Juggernaut, the false god of India.

29 Now the art of printing was not known among the ancients; for it was invented in these latter days, even in the fourteen hundred and fortieth year of the Christian era.

* *Office of the National Intelligencer.*

P.

30 It was the helpmate of Freedom, and when the light which it spread burst forth upon the world, it began to open the eyes of man, and to destroy the poisonous weeds that choaked the growth of Liberty.

31 Moreover, to complete the vandalism of Cockburn and Ross, they fell upon the printed books of the great Sanhedrim.

32 Even those that had been gathered together for instruction; the toil of many years; containing the learning and wisdom of ages.

33 And they consumed them with fire; thus striving to turn man back to the ages of ignorance and darkness.

34 Now, Thomas, whose sir-name was JEFFERSON, who had been a scribe in the days of WASHINGTON, and a chief governor in the land of Columbia, in times past; a man whom the people esteemed for his virtue;

35 When he heard of their wickedness; how, savage-like, they had burnt the books which had been written by the wise men of the earth, and preserved from the beginning to that day;

36 In the goodness of his heart, he wrote unto the great Sanhedrim, when they were assembled together, saying:

37 Since, like the barbarians of old, whose ignorance might plead for them, the servants of the kingdom of Great Britain have laid waste your chief city, and made it a desolation,

38 And have trampled upon science, mutilated the monuments of art and industry, destroyed the archives of your nation, and burnt your books with fire;

39 For your benefit, and for the benefit of my country, I will give unto you my whole Library, which I have selected with care, from my youth upwards; and whatever in your judgment shall be the value thereof, that will I accept.*

40 I am well stricken in years, and must shortly sleep with my fathers; but the last wish of my heart shall be the WELFARE OF MY COUNTRY.

41 Now Thomas was a Philosopher, and a man of great learning, and he had abundance of books of all nations, and in all languages, even ten thousand volumes.

42 So the great Sanhedrim accepted the offer of Thomas, and they retain the books to this day.

43 Now it came to pass, in the evening of the same day, on which the vandals of Britain set fire to the city, that the army of the king fled from the place; for the air of Liberty is poison to the followers of tyrants.

44 Moreover, they left some of their slain and wounded behind, for they were afraid of being caught in a snare by the hushandmen of Columbia.

45 So they went down to the river and gat into their vessels from whence they came.

46 In the meantime, the inhabitants of Alexandria, a town which lieth to the south of the chief city, on the river Potowmac, in the state of Virginia,

---

* Mr. Jefferson left it to Congress to make him what compensation they thought proper for his Library.

47 Being smitten with fear, sent to Cockburn and Ross, entreating that they might be spared, if, peradventure, they made a covenant in good faith with them, and surrendered themselves.

48 And the chief captains of Britain agreed to the capitulation of the town, and to vouchsafe its protection.

49 But the people suffered for their foolish confidence ; and no one pitied them ; for it was of their own seeking.

50 So it happened, after they had trusted to the faith of the servants of the king ; Gordon, a captain of the ships in the river Potowmac, came up against them before the town ;

51 And took their merchant ships ; and compelled the people to open their store-houses, and put into the vessels their flour, even sixteen thousand barrels, and their wine, and their cotton, and a thousand hogsheads of the sweet-scented plant.

52 So the robbers of the king took them away, sacked the town, and laughed at the people thereof, for trusting to the faith of British honour.

53 However, as they passed along down the river, with their ill-gotten treasure, lo! the ships of Britain were assailed, and nigh being destroyed :

54 For Rogers, and Perry, and Porter, three valiant captains of the navy of Columbia, gave them hindrance and annoyed them greatly :

55 Perry and Porter raised fortifications upon the borders of the river, and put therein the destroying

engines, which, when the vessels came nigh by, they let loose upon them abundantly, and wounded them in their tackling, and slew numbers of their men.

56 Moreover, the balls which the engines vomited forth, were red and hot from the mouth of the fiery furnace.

57 Meanwhile, Rogers sent his fire-ships among them to destroy them as they fled; nevertheless they escaped.

58 Now about this time, being the thirtieth day of the same month, Peter, whose sir-name was Parker, who commanded a strong ship of the king, was committing many depredations along the shores of the Chesapeake;

59 So Peter essayed to go, in the night-time, against some of the husbandmen of Columbia, commanded by the gallant Reid,* about the borders of the state of Maryland;

60 And when he had landed his men of war, he went out after the husbandmen, and the plunder; but they were upon the watch, and fell upon him, and killed and maimed about two score, and were nigh making captives of them all; and Peter was amongst the slain.

61 Now when the news of the taking of the chief city of Columbia, and the sacking of Alexandria was

---

* Col Reid, of the militia.

received in Britain, at first the people rejoiced, saying, 'Now, forsooth, have we conquered these cunning Yankees!

62 But afterwards they became ashamed, and hid their faces; for they had heard the judgment of the surrounding nations, by whom their vandalism was condemned.*

---

* *A number of well written articles were published, not only in the papers of France and Germany, but even in England, in which this scandalous imitation of the conduct of the Goths and Vandals was very severely reprehended.*

CHAP. XLVI.

British under Gen. Prevost, go against Plattsburgh —Com. Macdonough captures the British squadron on Lake Champlain.

———

NEVERTHELESS, if difficulties and disasters befel the people of Columbia in the south, lo! there was a wreath of laurels weaving for them in the north.

2 Behold! a mighty army of the king had assembled together at the village of Champlain, between Plattsburgh and Montreal; nigh unto the place where Forsyth the warrior, the second Sumter,* was slain:

3 For the Prince Regent had commanded his servants to go forth into the heart of the land of Colum-

———

* *Sumter, a brave officer in the American Revolution, similar in character to Forsyth.*

The following lines were suggested to the mind of the writer, by viewing the spot where the remains of the gallant Forsyth lie interred. On the 28th of June, 1814, this enterprising officer made an incursion into Canada as far as Odlestown, where an affair took place with a detachment of the enemy from the Port of La Cole. After killing seventeen of their number, Forsyth recieved a wound in the neck of which he died

bia, and separate the states of the east from the rest of the country.

4 So it came to pass, about the fifth day of the ninth month, that the host of Britain appeared before the village of -Plattsburgh; which lieth about three hundred miles from New-York, towards the north.

5 Now Prevost, the governor of Canada, was the commander of the army; and the number of his men of war was about fifteen thousand.

6 And they began to prepare their battering rams, their bombs, and their rockets, and all kinds of instruments of destruction; and they entrenched themselves round about.

7 Now the strong hold of Plattsburgh was hard by; and the barve Macomb was the chief captain of

------

in a few days after, and was buried, with military ho-
nors, at Champlain.

     Stop, traveller, stay—view well the ground
        Where Forsyth fought and bled;
     Mark well the spot, for yonder mound,
        Contains the valiant dead.

     No *cold neglect* could check *his* zeal,
        His Country was his pride,
     And fighting for that Country's weal,
        The hero nobly died!

     No tomb-stone marks the dreary spot,
        Where sleeps the warrior brave;
     His fame, his actions, quite forgot,
        And buried in his grave.

the-hold ; and the number of his men was about fifteen
hundred ; being in the proportion of *one* Yankee *to ten*
invincibles.

8 Howsoever, the valiant husbandmen of the states
of Vermont and New-York, called militia, commanded
by Mooers, a man of great courage, assembled together,
to assist in the defence of the place, on the borders of
the river Saranac, which emptieth its waters into lake
Champlain.

9 In the meantime, Downie, the chief captain of the
fleet of Britain upon the lake, had prepared himself to
assist Prevost on a certain day appointed,

10 When he was to come out against the fleet of
Columbia, which was commanded by the gallant Macdonough.

11 Accordingly, it came to pass, on the appointed
day, being the eleventh of the ninth month, in the one
thousand eight hundred and fourteenth year of the
Christian era,

12 And three hundred and sixty-five days after Oliver had captured the king's fleet on the waters of Erie,

13 That the strong vessels of Britain appeared, with
their sails spread, moving upon the bosom of lake
Champlain, coming against the fleet of Columbia.

14 Now it was in the morning, about the ninth hour,
when Macdonough beheld the fleet of Britain sailing
boldly towards him.

15 And it was so, that the vessels of Columbia
were safely moored in the bay of Plattsburgh, where
they waited the approach of the enemy ; who were the
strongest in numbers, and in their engines of death.

16 However, when they were about a furlong off, they cast their anchors, and set themselves in battle array, squadron against squadron.

17 Now the sound of the battle-drum was heard along the lake, and the brave mariners shouted aloud for the fight.

18 Then began their destroying engines to utter their voices, and it was like unto the voice of mighty thunders.

19 And the same hour, the armies on the shore began the dreadful battle with their roaring engines.

20 So that on the land and on the waters the fire and smoke were abundant, and the noise thereof was tremendous beyond measure.

21 And the battle waxed hot, and the vessels of Downie fought bravely against the vessels of Macdonough:

22 Nevertheless, the Lord of hosts favored the men of Columbia, and they overcame the servants of the king.

23 For in about the space of three hours, the valiant Macdonough and his brave men, captured the whole fleet of Britain, save a few gun-boats, that made good their escape.

24 Now the killed and wounded of the king's fleet, were an hundred ninety and four; and Downie, the chief captain, was amongst the slain.

25 Moreover, the number of the captives of the men of Britain was about four hundred.

26 Now Macdonough was a good man, neither was he full of boasting and vain-glory: he arrogated to

himself no praise on account of his success, but ascribed the victory to the pleasure of the Almighty.

27 And as it is written, in the word of the Lord, DO UNTO ALL MEN AS YE WOULD THEY SHOULD DO UNTO YOU, so he took care of the prisoners, and employed skilful physicians to bind up the wounds of the maimed.

28 Then were the children of Columbia exceedingly rejoiced; yea, their hearts were made glad; and they praised Macdonough for his noble deeds.

29 Moreover, the great Sanhedrim honored him; and a piece of land, which overlooketh the lake, was given unto him, for an inheritance;

30 That, in his old age, and when he was well stricken in years, he might remember with joy the strength of his youth, and smile upon the spot, where fleet to fleet, he triumphed over the enemies of freedom;

31 And where his children's children might point, and say, It was THERE the guardian angel of Columbia permitted our father to humble the pride of Britain.

CHAP. XLVII.

*Battle of Plattsburgh——defeat of Sir George Pre-
vost.*

———

NOW while Macdonough was capturing the royal
fleet of Britain, upon the lake, the gallant Macomb
scattered destruction amidst the army of Prevost.

2 And the battle raged with great violence, and the
men of Britain strove hard to pass over the river called
Saranac ;

3 But the men of war of Columbia, who were upon
the opposite side of the water, opposed them, and slew
them with great slaughter.

4 And the brave Grosvenor, and Hamilton, and
Riley, and the gallant Cronk, drove them back from
crossing the bridges.

5 Likewise, many were slain in the river, so that the
waters of the Saranac were dyed with the blood of
the servants of the king.

6 But Macomb kept the engines at work ; and
Brooks, and Richards, and Smith, who were in the
forts, displayed much valor, and caused the engines to
vomit fire and smoke, and balls of heavy metal.

7 Howsoever, when Prevost saw that the king's
fleet was captured, he began to be disheartened, and his
whole army was amazed.

8 Notwithstanding this, they continued to cast their balls, and their rockets, and their bomb-shells, and their sharpnells, with all their might.

9 Now these sharpnells were unknown. even to the children of Columbia, for they were lately invented by the wise men of Britain.

10 But the people of Columbia trusted in the strength of their arms, more than in the strength of these shells, so they used them not.

11 Nevertheless, the army of the king fought hard, with their battering-rams, against the strong hold of Columbia, until the setting of the sun, when their noises were silenced by the brave band of Columbia.

12 So the same night, Prevost, and the invincibles of the king, fled towards the strong hold of Montreal; leaving their sick and wounded behind to the mercy of the men of Columbia; destroying their provisions, which in their haste they could not carry away.

13 And the men, of Columbia followed them a little way, and slew some, and made many captives.

14 Thus were the men of war of Britain conquered in the north, army against army, fleet against fleet, and squadron against squadron.

15 And the killed and wounded of the army of the king that day, were about a thousand men; and about three hundred who were tired of their bondage, left the service of the king,* and joined the banners of the great Sanhedrim.

16 Now Macomb received much praise for his bra-

* *Deserters.*

very ; and his name shall be remembered by ages yet unborn.

17 Moreover, he spake well of all the officers and
men who fought with him.

18 And Mooers, who commanded the brave husbandmen of New-York and Vermont, and Strong, the valiant
chief captain of the men called volunteers, had great
honor for their noble deeds.

19 Likewise, Appling, and Wool, and Leonard and
Sproul, distinguished themselves among the brave.

20 But when the news of the capture of the fleet, and
the defeat of their mighty army, reached the lords of
Britain, they put their fingers in their ears, that they
might not hear it.

21 Neither would they believe it ; but when they
found it was so of a truth, they were enraged out of
measure.

22 And their wise men and their counsellors said, Lo!
we have only been trifling with these Yankees ; now
let us send forth a mighty fleet and an army to over-
whelm them.

CHAP. XLVIII.

Attack on Baltimore, by the British army, under Gen. Ross, and the fleet under Admirals Cochrane and Cockburn.

NOW when Ross and Cockburn returned from their burning and pillaging, and all the barbarities they committed at Washington, the chief city, and the neighborhood thereof;

2 Emboldened by the success of their unrighteous deeds, they gathered together their army and their navy, and essayed to go against the city of Baltimore, which lieth in the state of Maryland;

3 That they might commit the like wickedness, in which they had taken so much pleasure at Hampton, Havre-de-grace, and Washington.

4 But they had a mightier place than Washington to go against; for Baltimore is a great city, containing therein about fifty thousand souls, and the people had entrenched it round about, and made it a strong place.

5 So it came to pass, the next day after Macdonough had captured the fleet of Britain, on lake Champlain, being the twelfth day of the ninth month,

6 That their vessels and transports came to a place called North Point, which lieth at the mouth of the river

Petapsco, about an hundred furlongs from the city, and began to put their men of war upon the shore.

7 And the number of their chosen fighting men, who were landed, were about eight thousand.

8 And when they were all moved out of the boats, Ross, the chief captain, conducted them on towards the city.

9 As they moved along their instruments of war glittered in the beams of the sun ; and the waving of their squadrons was like unto the troubled waters of the ocean.

10 However, when they came to a place called Bear Creek, lo ! the army of Columbia met them in battle array.

11 For, when the gallant young men of Baltimore heard the rumor, that the soldiers of Britain were coming upon them ;

12 With the spirit of freemen, they grasped their weapons of war in their hands, and went out to meet them without fear ; resolved to conquer or to die.*

13 For well they knew, that life would be a burthen to them, when their habitations were consumed with fire; their parents slaughtered ; and the innocence of their wives and sisters violated.

14 Now the name of the chief captain of the army of Columbia was Samuel, whose sir-name was Smith :† a valiant man, who had fought in the days of Washington, and gained much honor.

---

* *Although it may be said the British were not conquered ; yet they were defeated.*

Gen. Smith.

15 Moreover, Samuel was a man well stricken in years, and he had many brave captains under him; even Stricker, and Stansbury, and Winder were with him.

16 Now it was somewhat after the mid-day when the engines of destruction began their roaring noises :

17 And the fire and smoke were vomited forth out of their mouths, so that the light of the sun was hidden by the means of the black clouds that filled the air.

18 And their rockets, and all their instruments of death, which the sons of men have employed their understandings to invent, were used abundantly.

19 Now the battle waxed hot, and the gallant Stricker, and his brave men, fought hard : and it was a dreadful fight,

20 Inasmuch as the slain and wounded of the king that day, were about four hundred; and the loss of the men of Columbia was two hundred.

21 Moreover, Ross, the chief captain of the host of Britain, was amongst the slain ; a boy, who had accompanied his father to battle, had taken dreadful aim at Ross, with his rifle, and killed him :

22 And the people of Columbia grieved only because it was not Cockburn the wicked, who had fallen; for a man, whose name was O'Boyle, had offered five hundred pieces of silver for each of his ears.

23 Nevertheless, the men of Columbia were not powerful enough to overcome the servants of the king; so they drew back into their entrenchments, and strong holds, that were upon the high places round about the city.

24 And Rogers, and Findley, and Harris, and Stiles were among the captains of the strong holds; and were all faithful men.

25 But it came to pass, the next day, when the men of Britain saw that the men of Columbia were well prepared for battle, that they were afraid to go against the strong holds.

26 So in the middle of the night, which was dark and rainy, they departed from the place, and returned to their vessels, that they might escape the evil that was preparing for them.

27 Moreover, they took the dead body of Ross, their chief captain, with them, and cast it into a vessel, filled with the strong waters of Jamaica;

28 That the instrument of their wickedness might be preserved, and conveyed to the king, their master, and be buried in his own country.

29 Now it came to pass, in the meantime, that Cochrane, and Cockburn the wicked, the chief captain, of the mariners of the king, sailed up the river Petapsco, towards the strong hold of Fort M'Henry, to assail it.

30 Now the strong hold of M'Henry lieth about fifteen furlongs from the city; and the name of the chief captain thereof was Armistead, a man of courage: albeit, he was sick.

31 And when the strong vessels of the king drew nigh unto the fort, they cast their rockets and their bomb-shells into it plentifully, and strove hard to drive the men of Columbia away.

32. But the gallant Armistead let the destroying engines loose upon them without mercy; and they cast out their thunders, winged with death, among the servants of the king.

33 The loud groans of their wounded floated upon the waters, with an awful horror that shocked the ear of humanity.

34 And it was so, that when Cockburn found he could not prevail against the strong hold, he also departed from the river, neither came they against the place any more.*

One of the gallant defenders of Fort M'Henry has celebrated this circumstance in deathless verse. His poetry is so exquisite, and his descriptions so pathetic, that we cannot resist the pleasure of presenting his stanzas to our readers.

The Star-Spangled Banner.

O! say, can you see, by the dawn's early light,
    What so proudly we hail'd at the twilight's last
        gleaming,
Whose broad stripes and bright stars through the perilous fight,
        lous fight,
    O'er the ramparts we watch'd were so gallantly
        streaming?
And the rocket's red glare, the bombs bursting in air,
    Gave proof through the night that our flag was still
        there;
    O! say, does that star-spangled banner yet wave,
    O'er the land of the free, and the home of the brave?

35 Now when the men of Columbia heard that Ross, the chief captain of the king, was slain, and the host of Britain was compelled to flee from before the city, they were exceedingly rejoiced.

On the shore dimly seen through the mists of the
    deep,
    Where the foe's haughty host in dread silence re-
       poses,
What is that which the breeze, o'er the towering
    steep,
    As it fitfully blows, half conceals, half discloses?
Now it catches the gleam of the morning's first beam,
In full glory reflected now shines on the stream.
    'Tis the star-spangled banner, O! long may it wave
O'er the land of the free and the home of the brave.

And where is that band who so vauntingly swore
    That the havoc of war and the battle's confusion,
A home and a country, should leave us no more!
    Their blood has wash'd out their foul footsteps' pol-
       lution.
No refuge could save the hireling and slave,
From the terror of flight or the gloom of the grave,
    And the star-spangled banner in triumph doth
       wave,
    O'er the land of the free, and the home of the brave.

O! thus be it ever when freemen shall stand,
    Between their lov'd home, and the war's desolation.
Blest with vict'ry and peace, may the Heaven rescu'd
    land,
    Praise the Power that hath made and preserv'd us a
       nation!
Then conquer we must, when our cause it is just,
And this be our motto—" *In God is our trust;*"
    And the star-spangled banner in triumph shall
       wave
    O'er the land of the free, and the home of the brave.

36 And the brave defenders of Baltimore had great praise and honor given them throughout the land.

37 And the names of those who fell in the contest, are they not written on the monument which the gratitude of the people of Baltimore erected to the memory of its defenders ?

CHAP. XLIX.

*Destruction of the privateer Gen. Armstrong, Sam-
uel C. Read, captain—Scorpion and Tigress captured—U. S. frigate Adams burnt—Castine—
Fort Boyer attacked—destruction of the pirates
at Barrataria, by Com. Patterson—Gen. Jackson
captures Pensacola, and returns to New Orleans.*

Now the loud and frightful noise of war sounded
upon the bosom of the great deep; and the shores
of Columbia knew no peace.

2 The dreadful clangor of arms rung upon the land,
and echoed from the mountains; and the groans of suffering victims floated in the air of heaven.

3 But the Lord favored the people of Columbia,
and their armies and their navy gained strength, and
prosperity was showered upon them: the voice of
war became familiar to those who where strangers to
it in times past,

4 Now on the twenty-sixth day of the ninth month, being in the thirty and ninth year of American Independen-
dence,

5 It came to pass, that a certain private armed vessel of the people of Columbia, called the General
Armstrong, commanded by Samuel, whose sir-name
was Read,

6 Had cast her anchors in the haven of Fayal, an island in the sea, which lieth towards the rising sun, about two thousand miles from the land of Columbia ;

7 A place where, two score and ten years ago, there was a mighty earthquake ; and where poisonous reptiles never dwell.

8 And it was about the dusk of the evening when Samuel saw a number of the strong vessels of Britain hemming him in : so he drew nigh to the shore for safety, for the place was friendly to both powers.

9 Nevertheless, the boats from the vessels of the king went against Samuel to take his vessel ; but with his weapons of war he drove them off and slew numbers of them, so that they were glad to escape to·their strong ships.

10 However, they quickly returned with a greater number of boats, and about four hundred men ; and Samuel saw them, and prepared to meet them.

11 The silver beams of the moon danced upon the gently rolling waves of the ocean, and the sound of the oar again broke the sweet silence of night.

12 But, when they came nigh the vessel of Samuel, the men of Columbia poured out destruction upon them with a plentiful hand ;

13 Inasmuch as they were again compelled to depart to their strong vessels with dreadful loss.

14 However, about the dawning of the day, one of the strong vessels, called the Carnation, came against the vessel of Columbia, and let her destroying engines loose with great fury.

15 Now Lloyd, who commanded the Plantagenet

was the chief captain of the king, in the place; and he
violated the law of nations.

16 So, when Samuel saw that the whole fleet of
Britain were bent on destroying his vessel, in defiance
of the plighted honor of nations, he ordered her to be
sunk.

17 After which he and his brave mariners deserted
her, and went upon the shore; and the servants of the
king came and burnt her with fire in the neutral port of
Fayal.

18 Nevertheless, they received the reward of their
unrighteousness, for much damage was done to their
vessels, and their slain and wounded were two hundred
two score and ten.

19 Of the people of Columbia two only were slain
and seven maimed!!

20 And the valiant deeds of Samuel gained him a
name amongst the brave men of Columbia.

21 Now, in the same month, the Scorpion and the
Tigress, two fighting vessels of Columbia, on lake Huron, were captured by the men of Britain.

22 Likewise, about this time, there were numerous
other evils that befel the sons of Columbia;

23 Inasmuch as a brave captain, whose sir-name was
Morris, was obliged to consume his ship with fire,
lest she should fall into the hands of the enemy; and
she was called the Adams.*

24 Now this was at a place called Castine, which
was forcibly occupied by the strong ships of Britain,

----

* *U. S. frigate Adams.*

and lieth to the east, in the District of Maine : moreover, it became a watering place for the servants of the king.

25 But when James, the chief governor, and the great Sanhedrim, knew thereof, they sent word to the governor, and offered him soldiers to drive them from the borders of Columbia ;

26 But, lo ! the governor, even Caleb the Strong, refused his aid, for he was afraid of the wrath of the king of Britain.*

27 (Now Caleb, in the Hebrew tongue, signifieth a dog ; but, verily, this dog was faithless.)

28 Moreover, it came to pass, about the same time, that the strong hold of Fort Boyer, being at a place called Mobile-point, was attacked by the strong ships of Britain.

29 Now Mobile had lately been . the head quarters and the resting-place of the army of Jackson the brave ;

30 But the enemies of Columbia had become tumultuous at a place called by the Spaniards, Pensacola, whither he had departed to quell them ;

31 So that the fort was defended by only a handful of men, commanded by the gallant Lawrence.

32 And the names of the vessels of the king, that assailed the fort, were the Hermes, the Charon, and the Sophie, besides other fighting vessels ; which opened their fires upon the strong hold.

33 Nevertheless, Lawrence was not dismayed, al-

---

* *See the letter of Sec. Monroe, and Strong's answer.*

R

though Woodbine,* the white savage, came in his rear, with one of the destroying engines and a howitzer, an instrument of Satan, and about two hundred savages.

34 So when Lawrence let his engines of death loose upon them, and had showered the whizzing balls amongst them, for about the space of three hours, they fled.

35 And the slaughter on board the ships was dreadful; and about three hundred of the men of Britain were slain, and the Hermes was blown out of the water into the air with an awful noise.

36 The loss of the people of Columbia that day, was four slain and five maimed.

37 About this time a band of sea-robbers and pirates, who had established themselves upon the island of Barrataria, were committing great wickedness and depredations; and were ready to assist the men of Britain.

38 But a valiant man, called Daniel, sir-named Patterson, went against them with his small fighting vessels,† and scattered them abroad, and took their vessels, and destroyed their petty establishment of sea-robbery.

39 Now it came to pass, when Jackson heard that Pensacola, the capital of West-Florida, had become a resting-place for the enemies of Columbia; and that the men of Britain occupied the place, and had built them a strong hold therein;

----

* *The celebrated Capt. Woodbine, of the British navy.*
† *Gun-boats.*

40 From whence they sent forth the weapons of war, and the black dust among the savages, to destroy the people of Columbia; and that the servants of the king of Spain were afraid to prevent the wickedness thereof;

41 Behold! he, even Jackson, went out against the place with a band of five thousand fighting men, the brave sons of Tennessee, and other parts of Columbia.

42 And it was early in the morning of the seventh day of the eleventh month, when the host of Columbia appeared before the walls of Pensacola.

43 And immediately Jackson sat the engines of destruction to work; and the smoke thereof obscured the weapons of war.

44 Now when the governor of the place heard the noise of the engines of death and the clashing of arms, he was smitten with fear;

45 Insomuch that Jackson, the chief captain, who with his army had encompassed the place, quickly compelled him to surrender the town, and beg for mercy; which was granted unto him and his people, even the Spaniards.

46 Now when the men of Britain saw this, they put the match to the black dust in their strong hold, and it rent the air with a tremendous noise.

47 After which they fled from the land into their strong ships, that were in the haven of Pensacola.

48 And Jackson, having accomplished his purpose, returned with his army, in triumph, to the city of New Orleans, on the second day of the twelfth month

CHAP. L.

*Steam-boats—Fulton—torpedoes—attempt to blow up
the Plantagenet—kidnapping Joshua Penny.*

———

NOW, it happened that, in the land of Columbia,
there arose up wise and learned men, whose cunning
had contrived and invented many useful things.

2 Among these there appeared one whose ingenuity
was exceedingly great, inasmuch as it astonished all the
inhabitants of the earth :

3 Now the name of this man was Robert, sir-named
Fulton ; but the cold hand of death fell upon him, and
he slept with his fathers, on the twenty and third day of
the second month of the eighteen hundred and fifteenth
year of the Christian era.

4 However, the things which he brought into practice
in his life time will be recorded, and his name spoken
of by generations yet unborn.

5 Although, like other men of genius, in these days,
he was spoken of but slightly at first ; for the people
said, Lo ! the man is beside himself ! and they laughed
at him ; nevertheless, he exceeded their expectations.

6 For it came to pass, that (assisted by Livingston,
a man of wealth, and a lover of arts and learning) he
was enabled to construct certain curious vessels, called
in the vernacular tongue, steam-boats.

7 Now these steam-boats were cunningly contrived, and had abundance of curious workmanship therein, such as surpassed the comprehension of all the wise men of the east, from the beginning to this day.

8 Howbeit, they were fashioned somewhat like unto the first vessel that floated upon the waters, which was the ark of Noah, the ninth descendant from Adam;

9 And that they might heat the water which produced the steam, there was a fiery furnace placed in the midst of the vessels, and the smoke issued from the tops thereof.

10 Moreover, they had, as it were, wheels within wheels: and they moved fast upon the waters even against the wind and the tide.

11 And they first began to move upon the great river Hudson, passing to and fro, from New-York to Albany, in the north, conveying the people hither and thither in safety.

12 But when the scoffers, the enemies of Fulton, and the gainsayers, saw that the boats moved pleasantly upon the river, they began to be ashamed of their own ignorance and stupidity, and were fain to get into the boats themselves; after which, instead of laughing, they gaped at the inventor with astonishment.

13 And it came to pass, that the great Sanhedrim were pleased with the thing, inasmuch as they directed a fighting vessel of Columbia to be built after this manner.

14 So a vessel was built to carry the destroying engines, even a steam frigate, and they called the name thereof Fulton the First:

15 And certain skilful men were appointed comism-

sioners to construct this new and dreadful engine of destruction.

16 And Samuel, a philosopher, sir-named Mitchel, a citizen of New-York, was one of the commissioners; also, Rutgers, and Morris, and Wolcot, and Dearborn, were other commissioners; and they all gave their services freely for the good of their country.

17 Now she was equipped with thirty of the engines of destruction; and the weight of a ball that they vomited forth was about a thousand shekels.

18 And, when the movement of the frigate was seen on the river, she was as a strong floating battery upon the waters, terrible as death.

19 And the length thereof was about an hundred cubits, and the breadth thereof thirty cubits:

20 Moreover, as they had no gophar-wood, they built the vessel partly of the locust-tree, and partly of the majestic oak that flourishes in the extensive forests of Columbia.

21 But it came to pass, when the wise men and the people of Britain heard of this steam frigate, they were seized with astonishment and fright; inasmuch as it became a monster in their imaginations.

22 And they spake concerning it, saying, Lo! the length of this wonder of the world, which hath been invented by these cunning Yankees, is about two hundred cubits, and the breadth thereof an hundred thirty and five cubits:

23 The number of her destroying engines is very great; and the weight of a ball which she vomiteth forth, is about a thousand five hundred two score and ten shekels:

24 Moreover, said they, she is prepared to cast forth scalding water in showers upon the servants of the king, which will deform their countenances and spoil their beauty :

25 Likewise, they have prepared her with two-edged swords, which, by means of the steam of the vessel, issue like lightning out of her sides.

26 And now, also, the cunning and witchcraft of these Yankees, these sons of Belial, these children of Beelzebub, have invented another instrument of destruction, more subtile than all the rest :

27 Yea, these are mighty evil things, and they are called torpedoes, which may be said to signify sleeping devils; which come, as a thief in the night, to destroy the servants of the king; and were contrived by that arch fiend, whose name was Fulton.

28 Now these wonderful torpedoes were made partly of brass and partly of iron, and were cunningly contrived with curious works, like unto a clock ; and as it were a large ball.

29 And, after they were prepared, and a great quantity of the black dust put therein, they were let down into the water, nigh unto the strong ships, with intent to destroy them ;

30 And it was so, that when they struck against the bottom of the ship, the black dust in the torpedo would catch fire, and burst forth with tremendous roar, casting the vessel out of the waters and bursting her in twain.

31 Now these torpedoes were brought into practice during the war, although the war ceased before they did

that destruction to the enemies of Columbia, for which they were intended.

32 However, a certain man of courage and enterprize, whose name was Mix, prepared one of the torpedoes, and put it into the waters of the deep, at a place called Lyn-Haven Bay, at the mouth of the great bay of Chesapeake, nigh unto the town of Norfolk, in the state of Virginia;

33 And it moved towards a strong ship of Britain, called the Plantagenet, after one of the former princes of England; but an accident happened a little before it reached the vessel, and burst it asunder in the waters with a tremendous noise;

34 And spouted the water up into the air, as doth the mighty whale, and the sound thereof was, as it were the voice of thunder;

35 And the servants of the king were frightened horribly by the means thereof; after which they trembled at the name torpedo!—and were obliged to guard their vessels in the night, and put a double watch upon them;

36 Moreover, they condemned this mode of warfare, saying: Verily, this is a foul fashion of fighting; inasmuch as by your cunning ye Yankees take the advantage of us; and the thing is new unto us.

37 But they had wilfully forgotten, that in the life time of Fulton, they had offered him forty thousand pieces of gold, if he would bring these torpedoes into practice in their own country, that they might use them against the Gauls,* with whom they warred continu-

---

* *This was about the time of the Boulogne flotilla.*

ally for more than twenty years : Howbeit they proved faithless to Fulton, and so he did it not for them.

38 Moreover, it came to pass, that a certain man, a pilot, even Joshua, sir-named Penny, became a victim of their spite, because he attempted to go against them with the torpedoes to drive them out of the waters of Columbia.

39 Now Joshua lived at a place called East Hampton, being at the east end of Long Island, near Gardner's Island, opposite New London.

40 And the men of Britain came to his house in the night, and stole him away, even out of his bed, and carried him on board a vessel of the king, called the Ramilies, from whence he was conveyed to Halifax, in the province of Nova Scotia.

4 Now while Joshua remained in the dungeons of the king he was treated with the inhospitality of barbarians ; moreover, they strove to lead him astray : but he proved faithful to his God and to his country; for he had known the wickedness of Britain in times past.*

43 However, they kept him in bondage many months, after which they suffered him to go to his own country.

43 For the chief governor of the land of Columbia, and the great Sanhedrim, in their wisdom, had ordered

---

Joshua Penny had been, previous to the war, impressed in the British service, and kept in it a number of years.

two of the servants of the king to be taken and held as hostages for his safe return; and, but for this thing, they would have hanged him, even as a man hangeth a dog.

CHAP. LI.

Affairs in and about New-York, the first commercial city in America—working on the fortifications of Brooklyn and Haerlem—capture of the British tender Eagle, by the Yankee smack.

—

NOW, as good sometimes cometh out of evil, so the people of New-York, a great city, which lieth at the mouth of the river Hudson, nigh the sea coast, and containeth more than an hundred thousand souls,

2 When they beheld the wickedness that was committed by the servants of the king, to the south an d round about, began to bestir themselves, and prepare for the dangers with which they were likely to be encompassed :

3 So it came to pass, that the husbandmen from the surrounding country gathered together, and pitched their tents hard by the city.

4 And the number that came to the defence of the place was about thirty thousand valiant men; moreover there were about five thousand husbandmen from the state of New-Jersey,*

---

* *The exertions of Daniel D. Thompkins, governor of the state of N. York, at this time, will long be remembered by the people.*

5 Now these men were called Jersey Blues, and they were encamped partly at Paules Hook, and partly at a place called the Narrows, which lieth to the south of the city about an hundred furlongs, where the destroying engines were placed in multitudes.

6 And when the term of the engagement of these men of Jersey expired, they grieved only that their time was spent for nought ; for they were ready and well prepared to meet the servants of the king.

7 Nevertheless, it was so that the freemen who came to the defence of the city, built strong holds and forts, and raised up fortifications in abundance, inasmuch as the whole place was as it were one camp.

8 Moreover, on the tenth day of the eighth month, in the eighteen hundred and fourteenth year, the inhabitants assembled together in the midst of the city, even in a place called the Park, where the Federal Hall, a superb edifice, rears its majestic front ; within the walls of which the wise men, the expounders of the law, preside, and deliberate for the benefit of the people.

9 Now it was about the twelfth hour of the day when the people began to gather themselves together ; and, from the porch of the hall, the aged Willet,* with the star-spangled banner of Columbia waving over his silvery head, addressed the surrounding multitude.

10 And the people shouted with a loud voice, for the words of his mouth were pleasant to the sons of Liberty, and were in this wise :

---

* *Col. Willet, of New-York.*

11 Lo! three score and fourteen years have brought with them their bodily infirmities; but were my strength as unimpaired as my love for my country, and that soul which still animates me, ye would not have found me in the forum, but in the midst of the battle, fighting against the enemies of freedom.

12 Thus did he encourage the people to prepare themselves for the protection of the city.

13 And certain wise men were appointed by the people to bring these things into operation.*

14 So the people began to fortify themselves and entrench the high places round about the city.

15 And when they went out in its defence, to build their strong holds and to raise up their battlements; lo! the steam-boats of Fulton conveyed them thither, about a thousand at a time, even towards the heights of Brooklyn in the east, and the heights of Haerlem in the north.

16 The young and the old, the rich and the poor, went out together; and took with them their bread and their wine; and, cast up the earth for the defence of the place, freely, and without cost to the state.†

17 And when they went into the boats to cross over the river, there was loud shouting in the boats and on the shore.

---

* Committee of safety, composed of the Aldermen of the city, and their assistants.

† The services rendered on this occasion, by that respectable class of citizens, THE FIREMEN OF NEW-YORK, were particularly conspicuous.

18 Moreover, as they passed along up the Hudson, towards the heights of Haerlem, the fair daughters of Columbia, with hearts glowing with patriotism, waved their lily hands in token of applause.

19 Likewise, bands of men came from the neighbourhood round about; even from Newark, and Patterson, and Paules Hook, which lie in the state of New-Jersey.

20 They had also captains appointed over their bands; and Abraham and David were two among the captains.*

21 Now Abraham, with his band, came a great way, even from the town of Patterson, where the wonderful waterfalls pour headlong over the rocky mountains, reflecting in the sun a thousand brilliant rainbows.

22 Thus for an hundred days did the people of New-York prepare themselves for danger, and cast up entrenchments for many furlongs round about the city; so that the people of Britain were afraid to go against it.†

---

* *Major Godwin and Major Hunt.*

† *So great was the enthusiasm of the people in contributing their personal services to the erection of fortifications on the heights of Haerlem and Brooklyn, that scarcely could an individual be found in the populous city of New-York, from hoary age to tender youth, capable of using a mattock or a spade, who did not volunteer his services in this work of patriotism. Even the Ladies were conspicuous in aiding and cheering the labours of their Fathers, their Husbands, their Brothers, and their Children. Amongst others, the numerous societies of Freemasons joined in a body, and headed by their Grand-Master,* who was also*

* Hon. De Witt Clinton, now governor of the state of New-York.

23 Nevertheless the strong ships of war of Britain
moved upon the waters of the ocean around the place
in numbers, but they were afraid to approach the city;
for when they came nigh, the men of Columbia let the
destroying engines loose upon them, even those that

------

*Mayor of the city, proceeded to Brooklyn, and assist-
ed very spiritedly in its defence. On this occasion
an elderly gentleman, one of the order, who had two
sons (his only children) in the service of his country,
one of them highly distinguished during the war for
his wounds and his bravery, sung the following stanzas,
in his own character of Mason and Father, whilst the
Lodges were at refreshment:*

I.

Hail, Children of light! whom the Charities send,
　Where the bloodhounds of Britain are shortly ex-
　　　　pected;
Who, your country, your wives, your firesides to defend,
　On the summit of Brooklyn have ramparts erected:
　　　　Firm and true to the trade,
　　　　Continue your aid,
　Till the top-stone with shouting triumphant is laid:
The free and accepted will never despair,
Led on by their worthy Grand Master and Mayor.

II.

For me, whose dismissal must shortly arrive,
　To Heav'n I prefer this my fervent petition:
" May I never America's freedom survive,
　" Nor behold her disgrac'd by a shameful submission:
　　　　" And, though righteously steel'd,
　　　　" If at last *she must* yield,
　" May my sons do their duty, and die in the field?"
But the free and accepted will never despair,
Led on by their worthy Grand Master and Mayor.

vomited forth whizzing balls, like shooting stars, red from the fiery furnace.

24 Notwithstanding, the haughty captains of the ships of Britain would send in their boats to rob the market-men and the fishermen : howbeit, they were sometimes entrapped.

25 For it came to pass, upon a certain day, that the Poictiers, a mighty ship of the king, lying at a place called Sandy-Hook, sent out one of her tenders, even the Eagle, in search of this kind of plunder :

26 Whereupon, a fishing boat of Columbia, called the Yankee, under the direction of a chief captain called Lewis,* prepared herself with a number of men to entrap the Eagle.

27 So they took a fatted calf, a bleating lamb, and a noisy goose, and placed them upon the deck of the boat ; and when the servants of the king came nigh the Yankee, thinking they were about to be treated handsomely with the good things of the land of Columbia, their hearts were rejoiced ;

28 And they commanded the vessel called the Yankee to follow after them, towards the ship of the king, their master ; but at this moment the men of Columbia arose up from their hiding-places in the hold of the boat, and shot into the vessel of Britain.

29 At the sound of which they were so astonished, that they forgot to put the match to the black dust of

* Commodore Lewis, commander of the flotilla in the harbor of New-York—Sailing-master Percival gallantly conducted this expedition.

the huge howitzer, a destructive engine made of brass, which they had prepared to destroy the men of Columbia.

30 So they were confused, and surrendered the Eagle up to the Yankee.

31 And as they came up to the city, before the Battery, which is a beautiful place to the south thereof, the thousands who were assembled there, to celebrate the Columbian Jubilee,* rent the air with loud shouts of joy, whilst the roaring engines echoed to the skies.

32 Thus was the lamb preserved, and the proud and cunning men of Britain outwitted with a fatted calf and a Yankee goose.

* *American Independence.*

CHAP. LII.

*Affairs on the ocean—privateer Prince of Neufchâ-
tel—Marquis of Tweedale defeated in Upper Canada——Capture of the President—loss of the Sylph
——Capture of the Cyane and the Levant by the Constitution——capture of the St. Lawrence——capture
of the Penguin by the Hornet, captain Biddle.*

STILL there was no peace, and the evils of war
continued on the face of the deep, and the waters
thereof were encrimsoned with the blood of man.

2 And it came to pass, on the eleventh day of the
tenth month, in the eighteen hundred and fourteenth
year, that there was a sore battle fought between five
barges from the Endymion, a strong ship of the king,
and a privateer, called the Prince of Neufchatel, commanded by the valiant Ordonneaux, a man of Gaul.

3 Moreover, the number of the men of Britain
were threefold greater than the people of Columbia;
and the fight happened near unto a place called Nan-
tucket, in the east, journeying towards Boston.

4 Now they sat their engines to work with dreadful
violence; but in about the third part of an hour the
barges of the king's ship were overcome; and more
than three score and ten of the men of Britain were

slain and maimed: the loss in the privateer was six slain, and about a score wounded.

5 Now this battle happened in the same month in which more than a thousand men of the warriors of Britain, commanded by the Marquis of Tweedale, were defeated at Black Creek, in Upper Canada, and driven to their strong holds by the men of Columbia, under the gallant Bissel.*

6 Ten days after which the steam frigate, Fulton the First, was launched forth into the waters at New-York.

7 And it came to pass, on the fifteenth day of the first month of the next year, that one of the tall ships of Columbia fell into the hands of the servants of the king;

8 And she was called the President, after the title of the chief magistrate of the land of Columbia; moreover, she was commanded by the gallant Decatur,

9 Who, but for an accident that befel his ship the day before,† whilst he was moving out of the harbor of New-York, would have outsailed the fleet of Britain, and escaped, as did the brave and persevering Hull, of the Constitution, in the first year of the war‡

10 Nevertheless, it was so, that Decatur was, as it were, surrounded by the ships of the king, even five

---

* Gen. Bissel.

† She was injured by grounding off Sandy Hook.

‡ Commodore Hull, in this affair, gained much applause, for his manœuvres in escaping from the British fleet.

of them ; so one of the vessels, called the Endymion, fell upon him, and Decatur fought hard against her, and would have taken her ;

11 But the rest of the strong ships came down upon him, and opened their thundering engines, and compelled him to surrender his ship to the fleet of Britain.

12 However, it was a bloody fight ; and there fell of the men of Columbia that day twenty and four that were slain outright, and about two score and ten were maimed, after having kept the destroying engines to work about the space of three hours : howbeit, Decatur lost no honor thereby.

13 Two days after this, a strong vessel of the king, called the Sylph, was cast away, in a dreadful storm, at a place called Southampton, being on Long-Island, where more than an hundred men of Britain perished, in the dead of the night ; and the vessel parted asunder and was lost.

14 Moreover, there were six of the men of Britain who survived their brethren, and were preserved on pieces of the wreck, until the next day, when the neighbouring people took them into their houses and nourished them ;

15 And, when they were sufficiently recovered, that misfortune might not bear too heavy upon them, they were clad, and silver given to them, and they were sent to their own country, at the expense of the people of Columbia.

16 (Blessed are the merciful, for they shall obtain mercy, saith the scripture.)

17 Now it came to pass, in these days, whilst the fleet of Britain captured the vessels of Columbia, when-

'they caught them singly upon the ocean, that the single ships of Columbia began to capture the ships of Britain by pairs :

18 Inasmuch as it happened on the twentieth day of the second month of the same year, that a certain strong vessel called the Constitution, commanded by the brave Stewart, fell in with two of the strong ships of the king, and compelled them both, in the space of forty minutes, to strike the red cross of Britain to the stars of Columbia.

19 And the slain and wounded of the king's ships were seventy and seven; of the men of Columbia three were slain and twelve maimed : and the names of the vessels of Britain were the Cyane and the Levant ; but the Levant was retaken in a neutral port,* by two strong ships of the king.†

20 Now the valiant Stewart and his brave men gat great praise for their deeds, even the great Sanhedrim of the people honored them, and gave them twenty thousand pieces of silver.

21 In the same month the gallant Boyle, commanding the privateer Chasseur, captured the St. Lawrence, a fighting vessel of the king, in the fourth part of an hour.

22 And the killed and wounded of the St. Lawrence were thirty and eight; and the Chasseur had five slain and eight maimed.

23 Moreover, it came to pass, on the twenty-third day of the next month, that another fighting vessel of

---

* *Perto Prava.*   † *Acasta and Newcastle.*

the king, called the Penguin, was taken by the Hornet, a strong vessel of Columbia, commanded by a man of valor, whose sir-name was Biddle.

24 However, the battle was a bloody one, and the vessels kept their engines of destruction fiercely in motion, for about the space of half an hour before the flag of Britain was lowered to the stripes of Columbia.

25 And the slaughter was great; for there fell of the men of Britain two score and one: but the slain of Columbia was only one, and the maimed were eleven.

26 And Biddle was honored greatly for his courage:

27 But this was the last sea-fight of importance, being near the close of the war.

28 Now about this time the navy of Columbia had increased more than fourfold, and the fame thereof had extended to all nations.

29 For, though Columbia was young, even as it were in the gristle of her youth; yet she now began to resume the appearance, and display the vigor of manhood.

CHAP. LIII.

British fleet arrives near New-Orleans—the American flotilla captured—attacks by the British upon the army of Gen. Jackson.

———

NOW, when the lords and the counsellors, and the wise men of Britain, heard of all the tribulations that befel them in the land of Columbia, they were troubled in their minds.

2 And as they had made what they called a demonstration at Baltimore, they bethought themselves of making another demonstration in the south.

3 (Now the true signification, in the vernacular tongue, of the word demonstration, had always been familiar to the children of Columbia; but the new interpretation, although it wounded the pride of Britain, tickled the sons of Columbia ; for, as the world must think to this day, so they could only construe it, an ocular demonstration of British folly.)

4 So it came to pass, that they gathered together their army and their navy, even two score and ten fighting vessels, carrying therein about twenty thousand men of war; and the name of the chief captain of the navy was Cochrane; and the chief captains of the army were Pakenham, Gibbs, and Keane.

5 And they essayed to go against the city of New-Orleans, which lieth to the south, on the borders of the great river Mississippi, in the state of Louisiana, which, was covenanted in good faith, to the United States in the days when Jefferson presided as chief governor of the land of Columbia.

6 But it came to pass, that Jackson, when he had returned from the capture of Pensacola, where he corked up the bottles of iniquity that were ready to be empried out upon the men of Columbia,

7 Had arrived with his army at New-Orleans, he began to fortify the place, for he heard it noised abroad that the king was bent upon taking the city.

8 About this time, Jackson communed with Claiborne the governor, touching the matter ; and as his men of war were but few, the valiant husbandmen of Louisiana, Tennessee, Kentucky, and the Mississippi Territory, were informed of the evil, and accordingly they flocked in multitudes to the banners of Jackson.

9 Now, as Jackson and Claiborne had counted upon the arrival of the strong ships of Britain, so it happened, in the latter part of the eighteen hundred and fourteenth year, that they made their appearance, even in the twelfth month of the year.

10 And it was so, that when they had come as nigh as they could unto the city with their heavy ships, some of which carried an hundred of the destroying engines, they cast anchor :

11 And lo, after having passed a certain dangerous place called Pass Christian, they prepared their boats, containing more than a thousand men, and sent them

in great numbers against the boats of Columbia that were upon the waters of the lakes about the city.*

12 Now these small vessels of Columbia were commanded by Thomas, a brave man, whose sir-name was, Jones, and he gave them hindrance.

13 Nevertheless, in the space of about two hours, the boats of Columbia were captured by the vessels of Britain, one after another, until they were all taken: however, the mariners of Columbia fought well, and gained great praise; and the loss of the king was about three hundred.

14 Now the capture of the gun-boats of the United States upon these waters encouraged the servants of the king, so they began to land their mighty army upon the shores of Columbia in great multitudes from their boats:

15 And they pitched their tents, and cast up fortifications, and prepared to assail the strong hold of Jackson, the chief captain.

16 And, that the host of Britain might be discomfited at the onset, Jackson went out with his army against them; but the men of war of the king were twofold greater than the men of Columbia, so Jackson was unable to drive them away.

17 However, he fought bravely against them, and slew numbers of them; albeit, the slain and maimed of Columbia were about two hundred; so Jackson drew back to his entrenchments, and strengthened himself there.

---

* *Lakes Borgne and Ponchartrain.*

T

18 Now this happened on the twenty and third day of the twefth month, in the eighteen hundred and four-teenth year.

19 And it came to pass, on the twenty-seventh day of the same month, that a fighting vessel of the United States, called the Caroline, commanded by Daniel, was set fire to, and blown up, by the heated balls of the king's fiery furnace.

20 On the next day, the whole host of Britain gather-ed themselves together, and with their might went against the strong hold of Jackson.

21 But Jackson let the destroying engines loose upon the servants of Britain, and compelled them to return to their encampments with great loss, even an hundred and two score.

22 Nevertheless, on the first day of the first month of the eighteen hundred and fifteenth year, the men of war of Britain came again, and strove to dislodge the army of Jackson; but again they were deceived, and lost about an hundred men.

23 At this time there arrived to the aid of Jackson about two thousand five hundred valiant men, from the backs-woods of Kentucky.

24 Disappointed in their expectations, and failing in their attempts to discomfit the army of Columbia, the captains and the host of Britain arrayed themselves in their might to go against the hold of Jackson with their whole force.

25 And the morning of the eighth day of the month was pitched upon, by the men of Britain, for conquering the host of Columbia, and settling themselves in the land of liberty.

26 So they prepared themselves with their fascines, and their scaling ladders, and their bombs, and their rockets, and all the weapons of destruction that the ingenuity of Britain could invent.

27 After which Pakenham, the chief captain of the host of the king, spake to the officers and the men of war that were under him, saying,

28 Be ye prepared; for, lo! to-morrow, at the dawning of the day, our mighty squadrons shall rush upon these Yankees, and destroy them.

29 Here will we establish ourselves upon the borders of Columbia; and ye shall be officers, tythemen, and tax-gatherers, under the king, your master:

30 Moreover, a day and a night shall ye plunder and riot; and your watch-word shall be, BEAUTY AND BOOTY!

CHAP. LIV

Grand Battle of New-Orleans.

NOW Pakenham, the chief captain of the host of Britain, made an end of addressing the officers and the soldiers of the king :

2 And it came to pass, in the one thousand eight hundred aud fifteenth year of the Christain era, in the first month of the year, and on the eighth day of the month,

3 Being on the Sabbath day, (which, as it is written in the scriptures, THOU SHALT REMEMBER AND KEEP HOLY,)

4 That the mighty army of the king, which had moved out of the strong ships of Britain, came, in their strength, to make conquest of the territory of Columbia, which lieth to the south ;

5 And to place therein a princely ruler, and all manner of officers, the servants of the king, even unto a tax-gatherer.

6 So, early in the morning, they appeared before the camp of the men of Columbia, even the strong hold which Jackson, the chief captain, had fortified.

7 Their polished steels, of fine workmanship, glittered in the sun, and the movement of their squadrons was as the waving of a wheat-field, when the south wind passeth gently over it.

8 The fierceness of their coming was as the coming of a thousand untamed lions, which move majestically over the sandy deserts of Arabia.

9 And the army rested upon the the plains of Mac Frardies, nigh unto the cypress swamp, being distant from the city about forty and eight furlongs.

10 And it was about the rising of the sun, when the battering-rams of the king began to utter their noises; and the sound thereof was terrible as the roaring of lions, or the voice of many thunders.

11 Moreover, they cast forth bombs, and Congreve rockets, weapons of destruction, which were not known in the days of Jehoshaphat.

12 Nevertheless, the soul of Jackson failed him not, neither was he dismayed, for he was entrenched round about; and when he raised his hand, he held every man's heart therein.

13 And Jackson spake, and said unto his captains of fifties, and his captains of hundreds, Fear not; we defend our lives and our liberty, and in that thing the Lord will not forsake us:

14 Therefore, let every man be upon his watch; and let the destroying engines now utter forth their thunders in abundance:

15 And ye cunning back-woodsmen, who have known only to hunt the squirrel, the wolf, and the deer, now pour forth your strength upon the mighty men, that we may not be overcome.

16 And as the black dust cast upon a burning coal instantly mounteth into a flame, so was the spirit of the husbandmen of the backwoods of Columbia.

17 Now the brave men from Tennessee and Ken-

tucky set their shining rifles to work, and the destroying engines began to vomit their thunders upon the servants of the king.

18 Twice did the host of Britain, in solid columns,
come against the entrenchments of Jackson, and twice
he drove them back.

19 Moreover, Daniel the brave, who had raised up
defences upon the banks of the river, likewise let his
engines loose upon them, and shot into the camp of the
king.

20 And the men of Britain strove to scale the ramparts, and get into the strong hold of Jackson ; but the
husbandmen drove them back with great slaughter.

21 The fire and the smoke, and the deafning noise
that sounded along the battlements, were tremendous
for more than the space of two hours, when the dreadful roarings ceased, for the warriors of the king fled in
confusion.

22 But when the sulphureous vapors arose, behold
the battle-ground was covered with the slain and the
wounded officers and soldiers of the kingdom of Great
Britain !

23 Humanity shuddered at the awful scene, whilst
the green fields blushed.

24 Seven hundred of the servants of the king were
slain ; and their whole loss that day was two thousand
six hundred valiant men, who had fought under Wellington, the champion of England.

25 And Pakenham, the chief captain of the host
of Britain, the brother-in-law of Wellington, was
amongst the slain ; and they served his body as they
had served the body of Ross, their chief captain at

the Baltimore demonstration, preserving it, in like manner, with the strong waters of Jamaica.

26 Moreover, one of their chief captains, whose sir-
name was Gibbs, was also slain, and Keane was sorely
wounded : so that the charge of the host of Britain
that remained from the slaughter, fell to a certain man
whose name was Lambert.

27 The loss of the army of Jackson was only seven slain and seven maimed, a circumstance unparalleled in the annals of history : howbeit, there were about
two score slain and wounded upon the other side of the
river.

28 Now the whole loss of the king's army, from the
time they came against the country of Louisiana until
their departure, was about five thousand.

29 After this they were discouraged, for there was
but a faint hope left for them ; so they departed, and
went into the strong ships of the king, with their chief
captain *in high spirits.*

30 It is written in the book of Solomon, that a fool
laugheth at his own folly : now the men of Britain
were not inclined to laugh, for they were sorely grieved ; and, but for the fear of the laughter of others,
would have wept outright.

31 And Jackson, the chief captain of the host of
Columbia, gave great praise to the gallant Coffee, and
Carrol, and Daniel, whose sirname was Patterson,
and all the valiant men who fought on that glorious day.

32 Moreover, Jackson was honored with great honour by the people throughout the land of Columbia ;
even the great Sanhedrim were pleased with him, and
exalted his name.

33 And the inhabitants of New-Orleans were greatly rejoiced, and carried him through the streets of the city above the rest; and the virgins of Co lumbia strewed his path with roses.

34 For, lo! he had defended them from the violence of savages, who came in search of *beauty* and *booty!*

35 And when the wounded of the host of Britain, were brought into the city, the fair daughters of Columbia took their fine linen and bound up the wounds of the poor fainting officers and soldiers of the king, and sat bread and wine before them, to cheer their drooping spirits.

36 Now again were the servants of the king disappointed; for, as they were sent upon an evil, as well as a foolish errand, they expected not mercy.

37 And when they saw the goodness that was showered upon them, they said, Surely ye are angels sent down from heaven to heal the wounds inflicted by the folly of nations!

38 And should we again be led on to battle against your country, with propositions to violate your happiness, our swords, as by magic, shall be stayed, and drop harmless at the feet of VIRTUE and BEAUTY!

CHAP. LV.

Peace.

NOW after the fleet of Britain had departed from New-Orleans in dismay, they committed many other depredations of a petty nature.

2 In the mean time, Cockburn, the wicked, was busily employed in what his heart delighted; inasmuch as he carried the men of Britain against the borders of South Carolina and Georgia, and continued his system of robbery.

3 And here, with the strong ships of Britain, he captured a town called St. Marys, in the state of Georgia and, among other evils, he stole away the sable sons of Ethiopia.

4 And conveyed them to the island of Bermuda, of which the king had made him chief governor, and sold them, after promising them liberty and freedom.

5 However, it came to pass about this time, that the news of peace being made between the nations arrived in the land of Columbia.

6 For it had happened that the great Sanhedrim in their wisdom, had sent out Henry, sirnamed Clay, and

Russel, two wise men, called, in the vernacular tongue, commissioners, to join themselves with Bayard and Gallatin, who were sent before them, to try and make peace :

7 For the voice of the people of Columbia had spoken peace from the beginning ; they wished war might cease, and that the breach between the nations might be healed.

8 In the mean time the king sent some of his wise men to meet the wise men of Columbia, at a place called Ghent, a town a great way off, in the country of Flanders ;

9 For it came to pass, that the generous mediation offered by the emperor of Russia was refused by the council of Britain, who had not yielded to the voice of accommodation.

10 So, when the ministers of the two nations were met, they communed a long time with one another, touching the matter ;

11 But the ministers of Britain raised up difficulties, and demanded certain foolish terms, which, in the Latin tongue, were written *sine qua non*, and which being translated into the Yankee tongue, might be said to mean *neck or nothing*.

12 Nevertheless, in process of time, the wise men of Britain waved their demands, and agreed to the *sine qua non* given them by the commissioners of Columbia.

13 So a treaty of peace was made and signed by the commissioners of both parties, on the twenty and fourth day of the twelfth month, of the one thousand eight hundred and fourteenth year of the christian era.

14 And the treaty was sent to England, and confirmed by the Prince Regent, on the twenty-eigth day of the same month; for he was tired of the war, and saw no hopes of conquering the sons of liberty.

15 After which it was sent from Britain, across the the mighty deep, about three thousand miles, to receive the sanction of the free people of Columbia.

16 And the great Sanhedrim of the people examined the treaty, and it was accepted and confirmed by them on the seventeenth day of the second month, in the eighteen hundred and fifteenth year.

17 After which it was ratified and signed with the hand-writing of James, the chief governor of the land of Columbia, and published to the world.

18 Thus was a stop put to the shedding of human blood; and the noise of the destroying engines sunk down into silence, and every man returned to his own home in peace.

19 Now when it was known for a certainty that peace was made between the nations, the people throughout the land were rejoiced beyond measure.

20 And when the news thereof was spread abroad, the temples of the Lord were opened, and the people of Columbia praised God for his goodness; yea, they thanked him that he had strengthened their arms, and delivered them from the paw of the lion.

21 Thus did the children of Columbia praise the Lord in the strength of their youth, and in the days of their prosperity; not waiting till the cold and palsied hand of age had made them feeble, and robbed their prayers of half their virtue.

22 Henceforth may the nations of the earth learn

wisdom : then shall peace become triumphant, and the people of Columbia be at rest ;

23 And, as it is written, their swords may be beaten into ploughshares, and their spears turned into pruning-hooks.

24 But, nevertheless, if this war, like all other wars, brought evil upon the sons of men. it demonstrated to the world, that the people of Columbia were able to defend themselves, single-handed, against one of the strongest powers of Europe.

25 And the mighty kings and potentates of the earth shall learn, from this example of Republican patriotism, that the people are the only *" legitimate sovereigns"* of the land of Columbia.

26 Now the gladness of the hearts of the people of Columbia at the sound of peace, was extravagant ; inasmuch as it caused them to let loose their destroying engines, that were now become harmless, and set in motion their loud pealing bells, that sounded along the splendid arch of heaven.

27 Moreover, they made great fires and illuminations in the night time, and light was spread over the face of the land ;

28 And the beauty thereof was as if, from the blue and spangled vault of heaven, it had showered diamonds :

29 And all the nations of the earth beheld the glory of Columbia.

END OF THE HISTORY OF THE LATE WAR.

ALGERINE WAR.

American squadron sails from New-York—arrives in the Mediterranean, and captures the Algerine vessels—treaty of peace with the Dey—affairs at Tunis and Tripoli—Decatur's return to America.

———

NOW it came to pass, that while the war raged between the people of Columbia and the kingdom of Great Britain, other evils rose up in the east.

2 For the people who inhabited the coast of Barbary, even the Algerines, committed great depredations upon the commerce of Columbia;

3 Inasmuch as they captured their merchant vessels, and held the men of Columbia who wrought therein in cruel bondage.

4 Now these Algerines, who were barbarians, dwelt upon the borders of the great sea called the Mediterranean, in the way journeying towards the *Garden of Eden,* the cradle of the world; even paradise, where stood the tree of good and evil, and where the great river Euphrates emptieth its waters into the Gulph of Persia, which lieth about six thousand six hundred and sixty-six miles to the east of Washington, the chief city of the land of Columbia.

5 Moreover, the waters of this great sea washed the shores of ancient Palestine, the holy land, the place of our forefathers, and the country of Egypt, where the children of Israel were held in bondage forty years.

6 Nevertheless, the manifold evils which these barbarians committed, by the instigation of Satan within them, or by being led astray by the enemies of Columbia, raised the voice of the great Sanhedrim against them.

7 For they had violated the treaty which the people of Columbia had made with them in good faith, and set it at nought.

8 Now it had curiously happened, that through fear or folly all the nations of the earth had always accustomed themselves to pay tribute to these barbarians;

9 But the people of Columbia were the first to break the charm, with their brave captains and their destroying engines, many years ago.*

10 Howbeit, they were now again compelled to go against them, and strive to bring them to a sense of justice, if not by persuasion, by communications from the mouths of their destroying engines.

11 So it came to pass, on the third day of the third month, in the one thousand eight hundred and fifteenth year of the Christian era,

---

* *Alluding to the war against the Barbary powers, about 1804.*

12 That the great Sanhedrim of the people sent forth a decree, making war upon the people of Algiers, who were ruled by a man whom they called the Dey.

13 After which, the fleet of Columbia, which had been increased by the folly of Britain, was prepared to go against them; and the gallant Decatur was made chief captain thereof.

14 The number of the strong vessels was about half a score, and the names of the mightiest amongst them were called the Guerriere, the Macedonian, and the Constellation.

15 Now the name of the first of these tall ships was after a strong ship of the king of Britain, which was taken by the brave Hull, and burnt upon the waters; and the Macedonian was also taken from Britain by Stephen, sir-named Decatur :

16 And when they came into the waters of Europe, the men of Britain* gnashed their teeth with vexation, neither would they behold them, but they turned their backs, for their pride was wounded, whilst the surrounding nations beheld the fleet with astonishment.

17 Now it was on the eighteenth day of the fifth month, in the same year, in the after part of the day, that the fleet of Columbia spread their wings to the western breeze, and sailed from the haven of New-York ;

18 And, with Decatur, the chief captain, in the Guerriere, they bade farewell to the land of Columbia ;

---

* *At Gibraltar, &c.*

and the shouts of the people made the welkin ring, and their blessings followed after them.

19 And it came to pass, when Decatur, with the fleet of Columbia, arrived in the waters of the Mediterranean sea, being thirty days after he left the land of Columbia,

20 That he fell in with one of the strongest fighting ships of these barbarians, called the Misoda, and he followed after her, and in less than the space of half an hour, after letting his destroying engines loose upon her, he took her captive, with five hundred men that were in her.

21 And thirty of the barbarians were slain, among whom was their chief captain, whom they called Rais Hammida ; besides many were wounded, and about four hundred prisoners were taken ; but Decatur had not a man killed.

22 Moreover, on the second day afterwards, the fleet of Columbia captured another fighting vessel of the Algerines :

23 And the slain that were found on board, being numbered, were twenty and three, and the prisoners were four score : howbeit, there were none of the people of Columbia even maimed. Thus was the navy of Columbia triumphant in the east, as it had been in the west.

24 Now these things happened nigh unto a place called Carthagena, on the borders of Spain ; and when the Spaniards beheld the skill and prowess of the people of Columbia, they were amazed :

25 Immediately after this, Decatur departed, and went with his fleet to the port of Algiers, the chief city of the barbarians, lying on the borders of Africa.

26 But when their ruler beheld the star-spangled banners of Columbia, he trembled as the aspen-leaf ; for

he had heard that his strong vessels were taken by the ships of Columbia, and his admiral slain, and he was ready to bow down.

27 And Decatur demanded the men of Columbia without ransom, who were held in bondage; and ten thousand pieces of silver, for the evils they had committed against the people of Columbia: and the Dey had three hours to answer him yea, or nay.

28 However, he quickly agreed to the propositions of Decatur: and he paid the money, and signed the treaty which Decatur had prepared for him, and delivered up all the men of Columbia whom he held as slaves.

29 And the treaty was confirmed at Washington the chief city, and signed by James the chief governor, on the twenty and sixth day of the twelfth month, in the same year: and Decatur generously made a present of the ship Misoda to the Dey.

30 Now it came to pass, after Decatur had settled the peace with the Dey of Algiers, according to his wishes, that he sailed against another town of the barbarians, called Tunis;

31 For the governor of this place, who is called the Bey, had permitted great evils to be committed against the people of Columbia, by the ships of Britain, during the late war; inasmuch as they let them come into their waters, and take away the vessels of Columbia that were prizes.

32 So, for these depredations, the gallant Decatur demanded forty thousand pieces of silver, which, after a short deliberation, the Bey was fain to grant, lest, peradventure the city might, from the force of the destroying engines, begin to tumble about his ears.

33 From the port of Tunis, Decatur departed and went to a place called Tripoli, which lieth to the south thereof, where the brave Eaton* fought, and erected the banners of Columbia upon the walls of Derne.

34 Now the chief governor of the Tripolitans, whom they called the Bashaw, had suffered like evils to be done by the British in his dominions which had been permitted by the Bey of Tunis.

35 So likewise, for these evils Decatur demanded thirty thousand pieces of silver, but at first the Bashaw refused to pay it.

36 However, when he saw the strong ships of Columbia were about to destroy the town, he paid the money, save a little, which he was unable to get, and for which Decatur compelled him to release ten captives of other nations, whom he held in bondage.

37 Thus did Decatur, and his brave men in the same year, compel the powers of Barbary to respect the banners of Columbia.

38 Now, having accomplished the object of his expedition, he returned, encircled with glory, to the land of Columbia :

39 And all the people were rejoiced with great joy, and they made feasts for him, and extolled his name.

40 Moreover, the great Sanhedrim of the people honored him for his gallant exploits, and gave unto him and his brave officers and mariners, an hundred thousand pieces of silver.

---

* *Gen. Eaton, a hero of the American war with Tripoli, some years ago.*

CONCLUSION.

Commodore Bainbridge—Lord Exmouth's Expedi-
tion against Algiers.

— — —

IN the mean time, it had come to pass, that lest the
fleet of Decatur should not be sufficient, the great Sanhedrim sent out after him another strong fleet, commanded by the valiant Bainbridge.

2 But, lo! when his fleet arrived there, the peace
had been made, and an end put to the war by the fleet
of Decatur: so, after sailing round about the coast,
Bainbridge returned home again with the fleet of Columbia.

3 Now it came to pass, after Decatur had returned
in triumph to the land of Columbia, that the lords and
the counsellors of Britain became jealous of the fame
of Columbia, which she had gained in the east, in releasing her people from slavery, as well as those of
other nations.

4 Moreover, the barbarians committed depredations
against the people of Britain, neither did they regard
their royal cross, as they did the stars of Columbia.

5 So the king fitted out a mighty fleet to go against
them; and the name of the chief captain thereof was

Pellew, to whom the king of Britain had given a new name, and called him lord Exmouth.

6 Accordingly, as their movements were slow, in the fourth month of the one thousand eight hundred and sixteenth year of the Christian era, the mighty fleet of Britain weighed anchor, and shortly arrived before the city of Algiers, as the fleet of Columbia had done many months before them.

7 And it was so, that the chief captain of Britain, n the name of the king his master, demanded of the Dey, the men of Britain, whom he held as slaves, and also those of other nations.

8 But the Dey refused, saying, Ye shall pay unto me five hundred pieces of silver for every slave; then will I release them, and they shall be free.

9 And Exmouth, the lord of Britain, yielded to the propositions of the barbarians, and accordingly gave unto them the money, even more than twenty horses could draw;

10 For the number of Christian slaves which Exmouth bought of the barbarians, was about five hundred.

11 Therefore, the fleet of Britain succeeded not, as did the fleet of Decatur.*

---

* *Lord Exmouth has since, in a second expedition, succeeded in releasing all Christian captives confined in Algiers, and in obtaining the ransom money (to a very considerable amount) which the Dey had previously received from England and Naples.*

12 Thus, in this thing, did the lords of Britain strive to snatch the laurel from the brow of Columbia ;

13 But her valiant sons had entwined the wreath of glory ; and the scribes of this day shall record it, in ever-living characters, on the pyramid of fame.

FINIS

It was our intention to have expatiated largely on the subject of *Bible Societies*— of their importance, and unprecedented extension throughout Europe and America : but the limits of this publication prevent us from entering far on this subject, luminous as it is ; however, in time, another opportunity may offer : at present, the names of the officiating persons in America, by being inserted, may serve to show the respectability of this valuable establishment, which posterity will admire.

OFFICERS OF THE AMERICAN BIBLE SOCIETY.

PRESIDENT;

Hon. ELIAS BOUDINOT, L. L. D., *of New-Jersey*

VICE-PRESIDENTS,

Hon. JOHN JAY, Esq. of New-York.

MATTHEW CLARKSON, Esq. of New-York.

DANIEL D. TOMPKINS, Vice-President of the United States.

Hon. DE WITT CLINTON, Governor of the State of New-York.

Hon. SMITH THOMPSON, Chief Justice of the State of New-York.

Hon. JOHN LANGDON, of New-Hampshire.

Hon. CALEB STRONG, of Massachusetts.

Hon. JOHN COTTON SMITH, of Connecticut.

Hon. ANDREW KIRKPATRICK, Chief Justice of the State of New-Jersey.

Hon. WILLIAM TILGHMAN, Chief Justice of the State of Pennsylvania.

Hon. DANIEL MURRAY, of Maryland.

JOSEPH NOURSE, Esq. Register of the Treasury of the United States.

Hon. JOHN QUINCY ADAMS, Secretary of State of the United States.

FRANCIS S. KEY, Esq. District of Columbia.

Hon. BUSHROD WASHINGTON, of Virginia, Judge of Supreme Court U. S.

Hon. CHARLES COTESWORTH PINCKNEY, of Charleston, S. C.
His Excellency THOMAS WORTHINGTON, of Ohio.
JOHN BOLTON, Esq. of Georgia.
FELIX GRUNDY, Esq. of Tennessee.

SECRETARIES.

Rev. JOHN MASON, D. D. Secretary for Foreign Correspondence.
Rev. JOHN B. ROMEYN, D. D. Secretary for Domestic Correspondence.

RICHARD VARICK, Esq. Treasurer.

Mr. JOHN PINTARD, Recording Secretary and Accountant.

Mr. JOHN E. CALDWELL, Agent.

An account of the number of Bible Societies in the United States.

New-Hampshire,	1	Virginia,	15
Massachusetts,	14	North Carolina,	2
Vermont,	2	South Carolina,	4
Connecticut,	9	Georgia,	3
New-York,	66	Ohio,	11
New-Jersey,	16	Kentucky,	3
Pennsylvania,	12	Tennessee,	2
Delaware,	2	Louisana,	1
Maryland,	2	Michigan,	1
District of Columbia,	1	Missouri,	1

Total number, 168.

The number of these auxiliary societies are rapidly increasing throughout the world, and their good effects may easily be anticipated.——These, and the establishment of *Sunday Schools* in different parts of the United States, has had the most salutary effects, and every good man will no doubt give encouragement to that rich source, which opens a field to virtue, and plants the ever living seeds of a glorious immortality.

Where wisdom dwells, there virtue reigns.

DANIEL, D. SMITH,
BOOKSELLER & STATIONER,
NO. 190, GREENWICH-STREET,
New-York,

Has constantly FOR SALE *Wholesale & Retail* on the most reasonable terms a general asssortment of Books and Stationary (particularly School Books) among which are the following,) viz :

Bibles & Testaments	Guthries Universal Geog.
Spelling books, all kinds	Cummings do & Atlas
Psalms & Hymns	Goldsmith's do & do
Hartford Selection of Hymns	————————History of Rome Grecce & Eng.
Methodist Hymn books	Weems Washington
Baptist do	Am. Orators & Precep.
Common Prayer books	Columbian Orators
Walkers Dictionary	Dialogues for Schools
Johnsons do &c.	Monitors, Childs Instruc.
Ainsworths Latin & Eng.	Juvenile Expositors
Nugents Fr. & Eng. do	Murrays English Reader
Duifefs do do	Grammar & Introduction
Boyers do do	Murrays Key Exerciscs
Dufiefs Nature Displayed	————Sequel
Perrins Fr. & En. grammar	Expositors and Preceptors
Perrins Exercises	Dilworths Assistant
————Elements of conversation	Gibbons do
Greek Grammar	Key to do
Latin do	Dabolls Arithmetic
Clarks Introduction	Federal Calculator
Mairs do	American Selections
Ruddiman's Rudiments	Art of Reading
Eutropie	Childrens books
Jacksons book keeping and others	Primers
Ink Powder black & red	Blank books of all kinds
	Paper of all kinds
	Sand boxes &c. &c. &c.

What next?

Rogershaven Books publishes facsimile reproductions of books of historical importance and also original fiction and non-fiction titles. If you found this book useful or interesting and would like to help us produce more titles like this one, you can:

1. Sign up for our newsletter to get regular updates about our new titles at **RogershavenBooks.com/Newsletter**.

2. Leave positive ratings or reviews of this book online—it is available at all major outlets.

3. Spread the word by telling your friends about this book or by giving a copy to a friend or your local library.

4. Go to **RogershavenBooks.com/Titles** to find out about our library of available titles.

5. Email us at **Inquiries@RogershavenBooks.com** to share feedback, including about any out-of-print or public domain titles you would like us to consider publishing.

ROGERSHAVEN BOOKS